CAMEL HAIR TATTOO ART OF PAKISTAN

Analysis of its Symbols and Motifs

Afsah Idrees Akhtar

Camel Hair Tattoo Art of Pakistan

Analysis of its Symbols and Motifs

Afsah Idrees Akhtar

Common Ground Publishing 2016

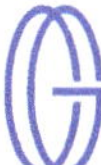

First published in 2016
as part of The Arts in Society Book Imprint

Common Ground Publishing
2001 S. 1st St., Suite 202
University of Illinois Research Park
Champaign, IL
61821

Library of Congress Cataloging-in-Publication Data

Names: Akhtar, Afsah Idrees, author.
Title: Camel hair tattoo art of Pakistan : analysis of its symbols and motifs / Afsah Idrees Akhtar.
Description: Champaign, IL : Common Ground Publishing, 2016. | Includes bibliographical references and index.
Identifiers: LCCN 2016024972 (print) | LCCN 2016031127 (ebook) | ISBN 9781612298887 (hardback : alkaline paper) | ISBN 9781612298894 (paperback : alkaline paper) | ISBN 9781612298900 (pdf)
Subjects: LCSH: Camel hair tattoo art--Pakistan. | Folk art--Pakistan.
Classification: LCC NK1051.A1 A38 2016 SF401.C2 (print) | LCC NK1051.A1 (ebook) | DDC 745.095491--dc23
LC record available at https://lccn.loc.gov/2016024972

To my grandfather

Muhammad Rafiq (1903-1993)

who instilled in me a passion for pursuing my dreams

Table of Contents

ACKNOWLEDGEMENTS

Special thanks to my mother who has been a beacon of light throughout my life. Her role has been all the more important for me since I lost my father at age 6. I am grateful to my loving uncles Roger and David for their constant encouragement in writing this book. I am thankful to my husband Muhammad Idrees Akhtar for his kindness and support. His knowledge of history and lively arguments helped me to explore from newer angles and make useful additions. I am grateful to my brother Bazil, sister Anila and brother-in-law Zeeshan, for their help in materializing this endeavor. I am thankful to my three children, sweet daughter Sumayyah who has been very helping in all the household works that got neglected while I was engrossed in this study, tech savvy son Haris for his technical assistance, and my young angel Hadi (he is not angel any more though!) for his affectionate looks when I was deeply engrossed in my work. They are the treasures of my life. They missed a lot while I was busy with this study.

I owe a special debt of gratitude to my teacher Dr. Shahida Manzoor who was a great source of inspiration in selecting this fascinating topic of camel hair tattoo art for my M.Phil. thesis. I am glad that she had the eye to see the significance of this study. I am deeply thankful for her encouragement and guidance throughout the writing. Whatever that I have learnt and contributed to the art of camel hair tattoo is due to her kind self. I am also thankful to Dr. Shaukat Mahmood for his ever so willing desire to help with a beaming grin. He has always been a support for me. I am grateful to Dr. Mamoona Khan for her fruitful discussions on the philosophical aspects of the book.

I am really grateful to my childhood friend Maria Amad who motivated me to convert my M. Phil. thesis in to the form of this book. A bundle of thanks to my dedicated student, Mohammad Shafeeq who accompanied me to far flung areas of Cholistan and made necessary arrangements in reaching out and finding the camel hair tattoo artists and for his marvelous photographic efforts. I am thankful to countless others whose names I am not able to recall now.

CHAPTER 1

Introduction

Although camels are abundantly found in many parts of the world, the beautiful art of camel hair tattoo is solely practiced in Pakistan and India. In Pakistan this art is concentrated in Cholistan though some artists can also be found in Mianwali, Layyah, Multan and adjoining areas of Cholistan (figure 1). In India this art is popular in Bikaner, Jaisalmer, Bijapur and some other parts of Rajasthan. This book primarily focuses the camel hair tattoo art practiced in Cholistan, Pakistan.

Figure 1: Map of Cholistan

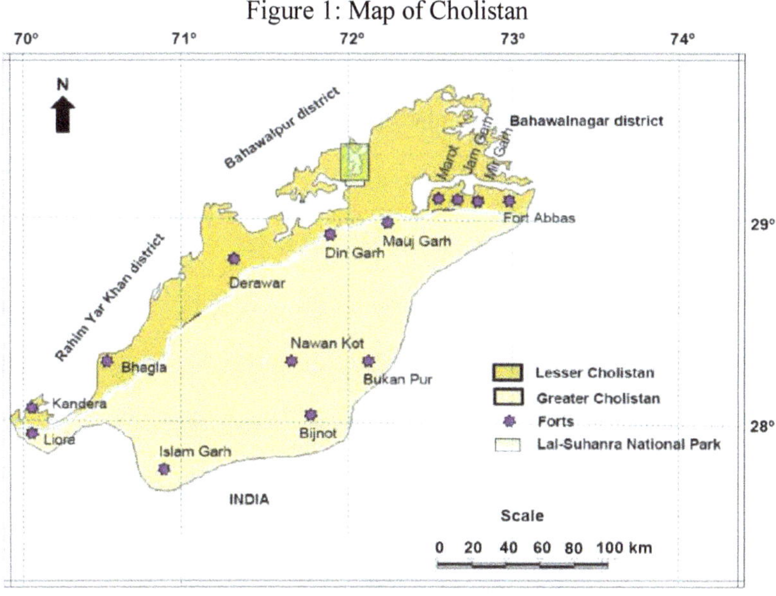

Source: Hameedi 2011.
http://www.pakbs.org/pjbot/PDFs/43 (SI)/07.pdf (accessed July 19, 2014.)

Camel hair tattoo art employs symbols and motifs and this book discusses their origins and meanings. The symbols and motifs of camel hair tattoo reveal ancestral roots in prehistoric rock art preserved in the caves of the adjoining areas in India, pottery of Indus Valley Civilization and the traditional Muslim art.

The artistic legacy of camel hair tattoo is a unique blend of art, philosophy and mysticism. This book explains artistic, spiritual, metaphysical and astronomical concepts employed in the symbols and motifs of this magnificent art form. Significantly, the spiritual aspects reveal that the art of camel hair tattoo is rooted in the Islamic beliefs, Sufism—the esoteric Islamic branch - and have some influences from other native religions including Hinduism and Buddhism. While the philosophical investigations verify camel hair tattoo as an art form with reference to metaphysical aesthetics, symbol theories, cultural aspects and spiritual links.

In this beautiful art form, the hair coat of the camel is cut to create various geometric and organic symbols and motifs (figure 2). The fur coat of camel is magnificently tattooed displaying an extravaganza of artistic, intellectual and mystical symbols (figure 3). The camel hair tattoo artist uses scissors as his primary tool to cut the hard hair of the camel. The lines cut across the fur coat display the artistry of geometrical forms covering the camel's torso. The tattooed lines in hair resemble the relief carvings of the wooden sculptures and the later application of henna dye accentuates the symbols and motifs to create a series of phantasms of subtle variations in color. In fact, the tattooed camel moving gently in the desert justifies itself as a piece of mobile sculpture echoing the inner spirit of a true artist.

Figure 2: Geometric and Organic Symbols and Motifs

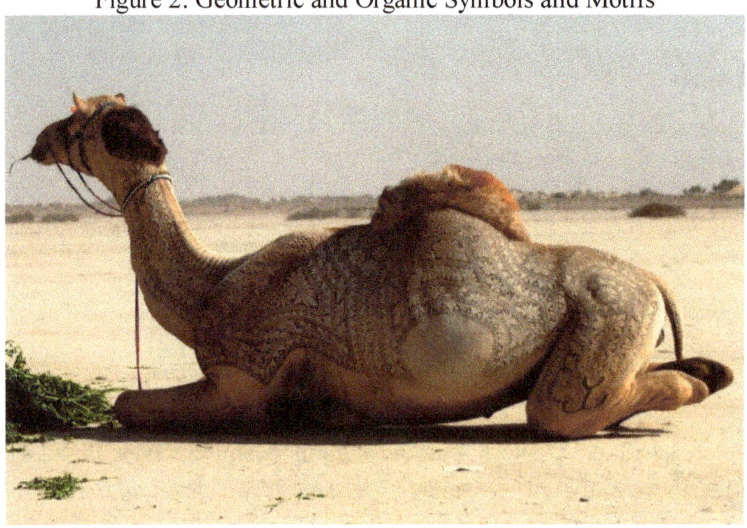

Source: Photograph by Muhammad Shafeeq, Channan Pir 2014.

Figure 3: Details of Symbols and Motifs

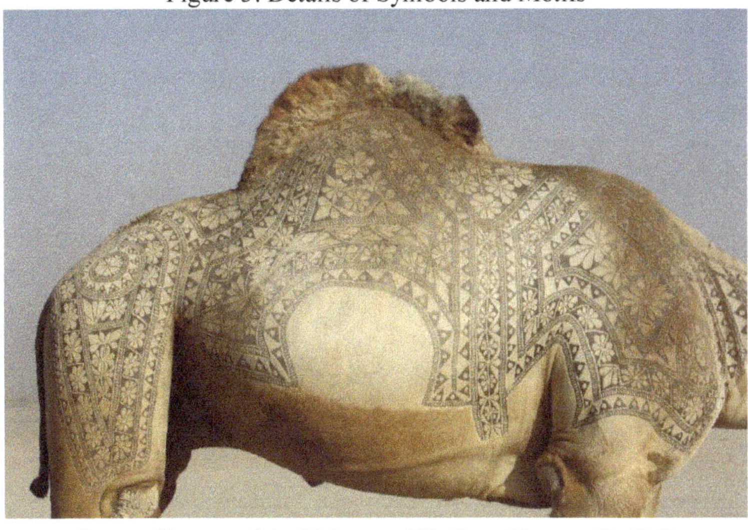

Source: Photograph by Muhammad Shafeeq, Channan Pir 2012.

The diverse symbols employed in the art of camel hair tattoo can be traced back to prehistoric times in the subcontinent. There are many cave paintings of the Paleolithic period, such as the Bhimbetka cave paintings in India, which reveal repeated use of similar symbols as used in the art of camel hair tattoo. The stick figures and larger animal drawings in these caves represent the sacred and secular practices of the ancient man. The history of these Bhimbetka caves, located 900 kilometers south-east of Cholistan in Madhya Pradesh, India, dates back to the part of the prehistoric times that was the fifth and the final phase of prehistory, marking the beginning of the agricultural age. Various zigzag lines, honeycomb and concentric square patterns within the body structures of the cave paintings of the animals have been painted in the fifth stage that highlight the importance of body decoration for the cave man (figure 4).[1] Following the centuries old traditions the present day artists of camel hair tattoo also use these multiple decorative lines to cut the coarse hair of the camel with superb inherited mastery (figure 5 & 6).

---

[1]. "India Netzone: Indian Monuments Bhimbetka Madhya Pradesh." http://www.indianetzone.com/10/bhimbetka.html (accessed February 28, 2014).

Figure 4: Animal Figure at Bhimbetka

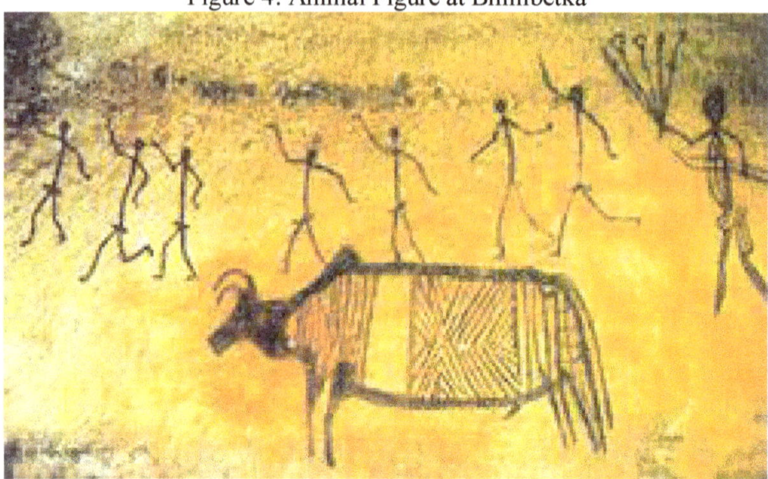

Source: India Netzone: Indian Monuments, Bhimbetka, Madhya Pradesh. http://www.indianetzone.com/10/bhimbetka.html (accessed June 21, 2014).

Figure 5: Zig-zag Lines resembles the Animal Figure at Bhimbetka

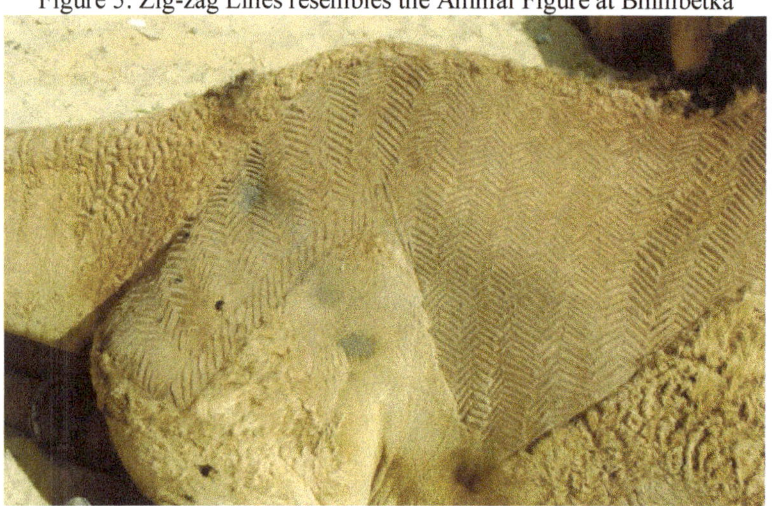

Source: Photograph by Muhammad Shafeeq, Channan Pir, Cholistan. 2014

Figure 6: Camel Hair Tattoo Lineation

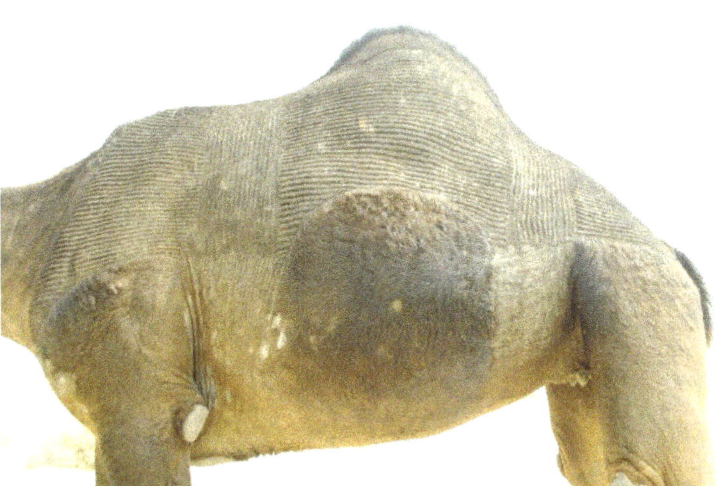

Source: Photograph by Muhammad Shafeeq, Marut, Cholistan. 2014

The desert of Cholistan was once a cradle of ancient Indus Valley Civilization which was one of the oldest and finest art producing centers in the ancient world. The most renowned cultural and artistic capitals of the Indus Valley Civilization are considered to be Harappa and Mohenjodaro and interestingly Cholistan lies in the middle of both of these. Another center of the Indus Valley Civilization Mehrgarh, about 500 kilometers west of Cholistan, is considered to be the oldest having existed during the period 7000 B.C. to 5500 B.C. Mohenjodaro was a beautifully planned locality which was 400 kilometers south-west of Cholistan while Harappa existed 300 kilometers north of Cholistan. The use of the dynamic lines and symbols can also be seen in the pottery of the Indus Valley Civilization particularly excavated from Mehrgarh and Harappa (figure 7).

Figure 7. River Hakra or Saraswati

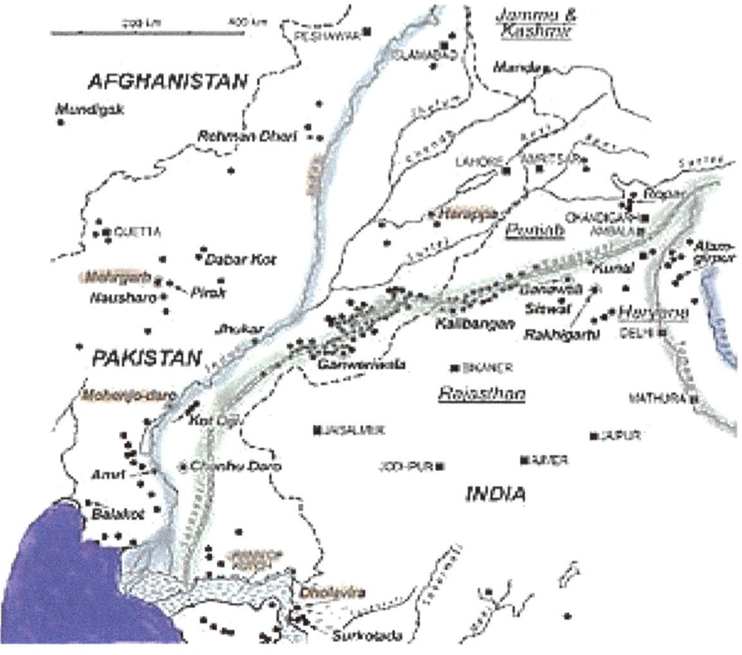

Source: http://manashsubhaditya.blogspot.com/2012_01_22_arChive.html_(accessed July 20, 2013).

In a major work, Muhammad Rafique Mughal, a prominent archaeologist on Cholistan, described in *Ancient Cholistan: Archaeology and Architecture* that the systematic survey of ancient sites and monuments of the south-east Punjab, Pakistan was undertaken with particular attention to the dried Hakra River. Cholistan is the extension of the Thar or Great Indian Desert bordering the Bikaner and Jaisalmer districts of the Rajasthan State in India. Its north-western parts are comparatively flat with small sand dunes scattered across the landscape and is known as the Lesser or Smaller Cholistan. The other area which is occupied by sand dunes of gradual rise with enormous height, which in some places are more than 500 feet high, is known as the Greater Cholistan. The western fringes of the Thar Desert or the Cholistan portion of Bahawalpur can easily be defined by the dry bed of Hakra River, also called the "Hakra Depression." The Hakra, which is known as Ghaggar in India and often identified with the sacred Sarasvati River of the Vedic Aryans, ran along the western edge of the Thar Desert and turned south into the eastern Sind and fell in to the Arabian Sea in the Rann of Kutch. The Hakra River was a perennial river until about the middle of the third millennium B.C. before its water was captured by the Yamuna River due to the natural reasons.[2]

According to Nurul Zaman Auj, the word Cholistan has been derived from the Turkish word, *chol* meaning desert. The ancient invaders from south-eastern Iran now called the Balochis brought the name with them. Cholistan's other name Rohi comes from the Pushto word *roh* meaning waste sand or a sandy desert. Pushto is widely spoken in the north-western province of Pakistan named Khyber Pakhtunkhwa and neighboring Afghanistan. In harmony with Rohi, its native is called a Ruhila. The Ruhilas of Cholistan seems to be of Dravidian origin; both having great similarities in their customs and traditions. The Dravidians are considered to be the original inhabitants of the subcontinent before the advent of Aryans about 3500 years ago. The invasions of early Aryans and later Jats, Balochis and Iranians did not change much the socio-cultural conditions of Ruhilas. The hard living conditions that prevailed after the drying of the Hakra River did not allow these foreigners to stay long and thus, leaving an uninterrupted and deep rooted ancestral links.[3]

The two surviving species of the camel in the western world are dromedary (camelus dromedarius) and Bactrian camels (camelus bactrianus) belonging to Arabia and Central Asia respectively. The dromedaries are also called the Arabian or the Indian camels (figure 8). There are two main breeds of dromedary camels in Cholistan and both are distinguishable on their characteristics. *Marricha* or *Marrichi* (also called *Mahra*) breed is used for riding and dancing and is used in hair tattoo art and the other *Barilla* or *Barilli* (also called *Milch*) breed has a short height a heavy body and is generally used for milking.[4]

---

[2]. Muhammad Rafique Mughal, *Ancient Cholistan: Archaeology and Architecture* (Lahore: Ferozsons, 1997), 20.

[3]. Nurul Zaman Ahmad Auj, *Harappan Heritage* (Multan: Caravan Book Centre, 1998), 72-73.

[4]. Mohammad Shafeeq Chaudhry and Umer Farooq, "Camel Rearing in Cholistan Desert of Pakistan," Pakistan Veterinary Journal, no. 29, (2009): 86-87, http://pvj.com.pk/pdf-files/29_2/85-92.pdf (accessed August 20, 2014).

Figure 8. Dromedary camels

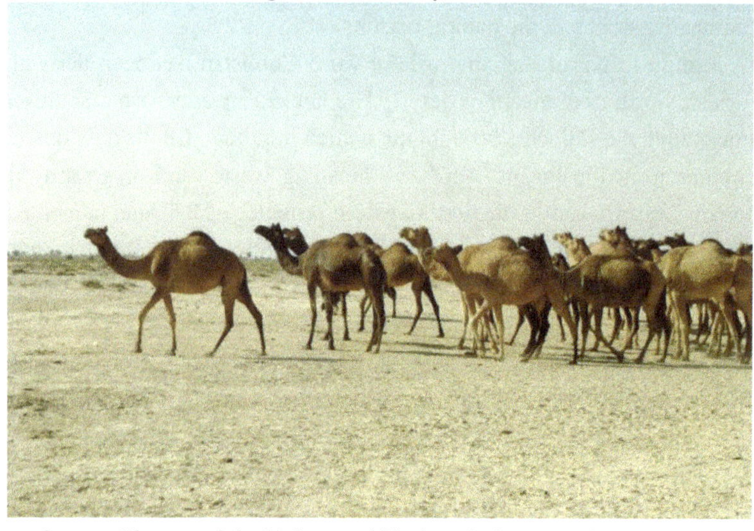

Source: Photograph by Muhammad Shafeeq, Kalay Par, Cholistan 2013.

Marricha or *Marrichi* camels vary from nearly white to almost black in color. The commonly seen camels of this breed have yellow-brown tones while the white and black colors are rare. The hair is lighter as compared to the skin. When the hair cutting starts the darker color shades of skin begin to appear from underneath. The black camels when tattooed show light brown while the ordinary yellowish camels show dark brown tones appearing from the hair cut lines. The lower parts of belly and the limbs which are in frequent contact with the sand during seated posture show dark marks of sand scratching. The artists cut the motifs in the hair coat with an astounding sense of color composition leaving some empty spaces for sand marks, bridles and howdahs.

The popular centers of camel hair tattoo in Cholistan are Bahawalpur City, Head Rajkan, Shahiwala, Tailwala Bangla, Mithra, Khutri Bangla, Qadi Wali Hattiyan, Miranian, Azam Wala, Kandha Farid Firuza, Rahim Yar Khan, Islam Garh Fort, Derawar Fort, Angtra Tubah, Din Garh Fort, Kalay Par, Moj Garh Fort, Khair Sar, Thandi Khui, Marut Fort, Marut, Kura Khuh near Ahmad Pur East, Hatayji near Mubarakpur, Basti Wani near Uch, Khan Pur, Basti Dar Khan near Liaqat Pur, Latan Shighar near Yazman and Channan Pir.[5] The places in Cholistan significantly focused in this book are Channan Pir, Latan Har Shinghar,

---

[5]. Mohammad Shafeeq Chaudhry, "The Art of Camel Hair tattoo in Cholistan, Punjab, Pakistan." *International Journal of Scientific and Research Publications,* no.4, (September 2014), http://www.ijsrp.org/research-journal-0914.php (accessed October 25, 2014).

Derawar Fort, Ahmad Pur, Uch, Kalay Par, Marut, Chak 11 and Chak 13 of Bahawalpur City.

Mianwali and Layyah in Pakistan are also famous for the festivals where camel related activities take place. (The festivals of Mianwali and Layyah are discussed in more details in the coming pages.) In the neighboring Rajasthan, India the most popular center is Bikaner where a popular camel festival is celebrated in January every year. The competitions of camel racing, dancing, milking, hair tattooing, etc. are much similar to those held in the festivals in Pakistan. These festivals also serve the purpose of attracting tourism. These desert natives feel pleasure and inner satisfaction by participating in such cultural activities. In Pakistan, the camels are trained in the art of dancing, racing, fighting and playing tricks to participate in various competitions held throughout the year. Ideally, the most suitable age for training a camel ranges from 2 to 4 years. As the camel grows mature in habits the trainer finds it difficult to mold. Well trained camels are sold out at high prices in the market. The average price of a trained camel ranges from 200,000 to 400,000 Pakistani rupees (2000 to 4000 U.S. dollars) depending on camel's health, age and the level of its mastery over various skills of dancing and racing. One single camel can be adept in the skills of dancing, racing and riding.

The Ruhilas put a lot more personal efforts to take good care of their beloved camels. During the winter season, they spend a lot on camels and feed them with almonds and local herbal medications to protect them from cold weather in the desert. The camel owners put camels to no work in the months of December and January for the fear of catching any disease. From the end of February to the beginning of March the weather conditions become favorable to resume the camel activities including camel hair tattoo.

The only festival celebrated in the beginning of winter season is the popular Latan Har Shinghar at Latan near Yazman, about 32 kilometers from Bahawalpur. It focuses the traditional camel riding competitions on the eve of yearly celebrations of the Sufi saint named Hazrat Qaim Hussain Malang Nurani Shirazi (figure 9). Similarly, the other popular festivals of Cholistan include Channan Pir Maila—which is the largest of them all in Cholistan, Marut Maila 304, Maila Walar Bangla, Maila Fort Abbas, Mithra Bangla Maila and Yazman Maila. *Maila* in local language means traditional festival or fair.

Figure 9. Camel Riding Competition

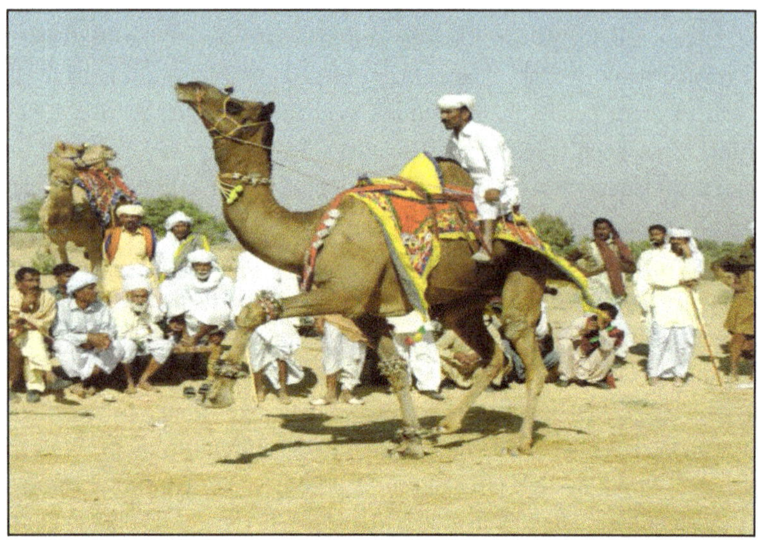

Source: Photograph by Muhammad Shafeeq, Latan Har Shinghar, Cholistan 2013.

The largest festival regarding camel activities in Pakistan, which is considered to be even larger than the Channan Pir Maila, is held in the city of Layyah every year. It is celebrated in honor of the thirteenth century local sage named Sufi Inayat Shah Bukhari, the disciple of Lal Shahbaz Qalandar - a popular Sufi saint of Sind - which attracts many local and foreign visitors to the Sufi shrine and enjoy the beautiful display of hair tattooed camels. These camels are brought by their owners to display their beautiful hair tattoo art. Some foreign visitors sometimes show interest in purchasing these magnificent camels, particularly the Arabs who are known for rearing high value camels take interest in buying the racing, riding and dancing camels at exorbitant rates. The reason can easily be understood from the fact that the art of camel hair tattoo and camel dancing cannot be observed in the Arab world.

The other popular festival regarding camel activities is held in Mianwali which is participated by a large number of camel hair tattoo artists with their tattooed camels. The participating camels for these traditional festivals are mostly bought from various places of Cholistan such as Fort Abbas, Marut, Chawk Azam, Layyah, Mithra Bangla, Moj Garh village, Yazman and Bahawalpur City to participate in various religious and cultural activities. The most enthusiastic camel rearers in Cholistan are the Saraikis and Balochis unlike the Punjabis who are more interested in domesticating cows, goats, sheep and poultry. The inhabitants of Cholistan have been rearing camels for the past many centuries and take care to keep their breed pure.

Undoubtedly, a camel is the most prized possession of the Ruhilas. Besides milk and meat Ruhilas use the camel as a beast of burden. It is highly suited for the rugged desert life in the extreme climatic conditions of Cholistan. The social status of a family or a tribe is determined by the number of camels it possesses. The passionately interested ones have trained camels that can dance and also take part in traditional camel race. Since camel is dear to them they adorn the dancing camels by cutting their hair coat in different symbols and motifs. The more valuable the camel the more adorned it is. Although it is a docile and harmless animal but some natives use them for the cruel game of camel fighting (figure 10).

Figure 10. Camel Fighting

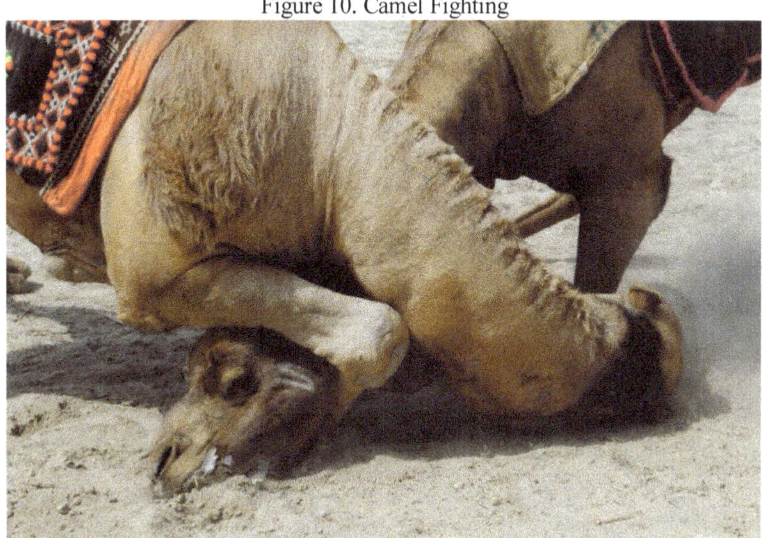

Source: Photograph by Muhammad Shafeeq, Jhok Farid, Cholistan 2012.

The adornment of camel is done with the art of camel hair tattoo in the spring season every year. As the spring arrives, the camel owners select camels based on their ability to dance or race. The ones that can do both are obviously more eligible. First, a local barber is hired to trim the long and coarse hair of the selected camel. The barber trims the hair with the help of a manual hair-trimmer to prepare an even surface of the hair creating about a half inch thick even base for the intricate motifs (figure 11). After the trimming, it is the job of the camel hair tattoo artist to cut the symbols and motifs in the fur coat of the camel.

Appropriate arrangements are made in the large and open courtyards of their homes for the camel hair tattoo artist who generally comes from far flung areas.

Figure 11. Manual Hair Cutting

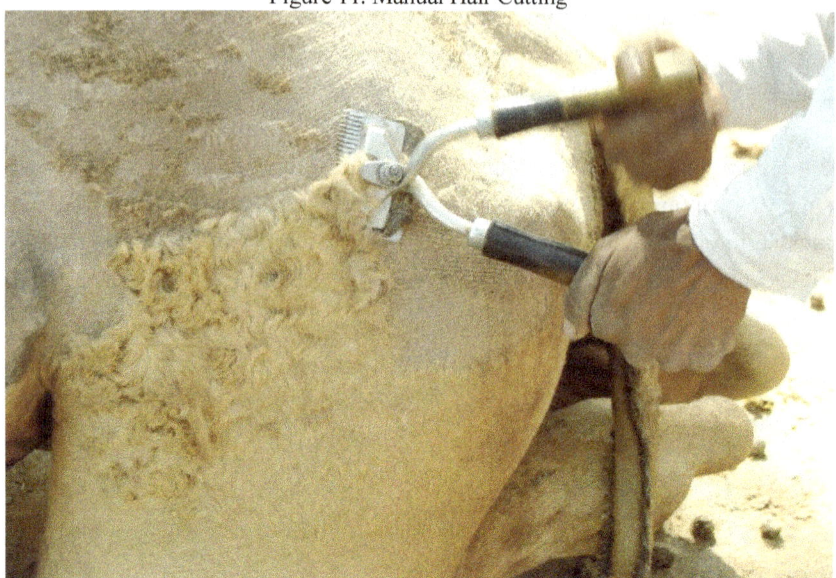

Source: Photograph by Muhammad Shafeeq, Miranian Cholistan 2014.

As a first step the camel hair tattoo artist marks some prominent areas of the camel including the hump, shoulder and back of the camel to begin with. The marking is done with an ordinary stationery marker which is followed by cutting a general outline of the motifs and patterns with the locally made steel scissors (figure 12). The artist keeps a number of pairs of spare scissors with himself. As soon as a pair loses its sharpness it is replaced with another sharp pair. The stock of sharp scissors helps the artist maintain continuity in his work without losing his rhythm and concentration.

Figure 12. Camel Hair Tattooing with Steel Scissors

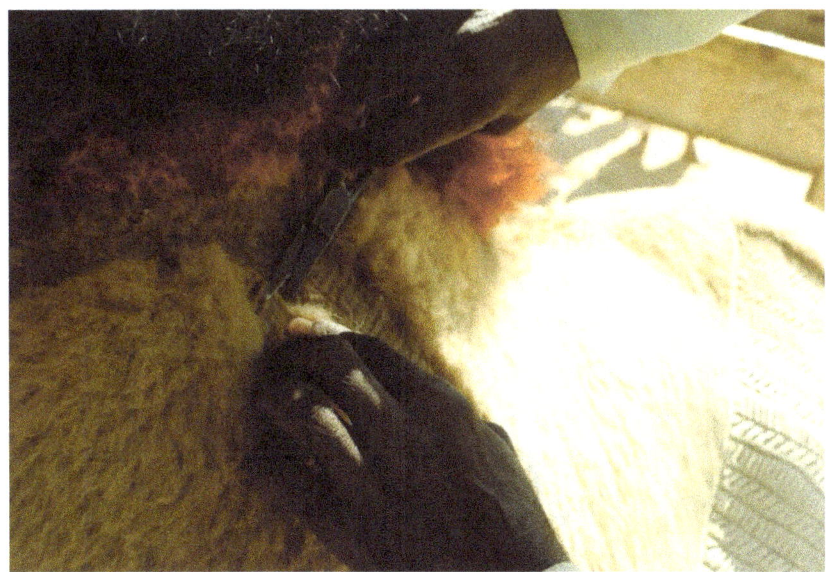

Source: Photograph by Muhammad Shafeeq, Miranian Cholistan 2014.

The artist cuts the camel hair along the complex anatomical and muscular structure of the camel including the head, neck, shoulder blades, hind limbs, belly and hump. With the assistance of a helper, it takes the artist about a week to complete the hair tattooing task and without any assistant the whole process may take up to fifteen days. More intricate motifs obviously demand more time. The assistant follows the outlines of the artist to cut the negative spaces in between the lines. The gigantic herbivore amazingly sits for hours, un-agitated and with ease and calm, throughout the hair cutting process. This perhaps is a unique characteristic of the beautiful Marricha breed.

The artist is a highly skilled individual and cuts camel's hair in varying lengths to produce different shades out of the hair coat, but the assistant is usually only allowed to cut full length of the hair along the camel skin that is as close to the skin as possible. After the cutting process, most of the camel artists apply natural dye of henna to accent the motifs (figure 13). Some artists also use hair dyeing oils like Kala Kola to get darker tones in the motifs. These motifs include the organic and basic geometrical shapes like triangles, squares and circles.

Figure 13. Camel Hair Tattooing with Henna Dye

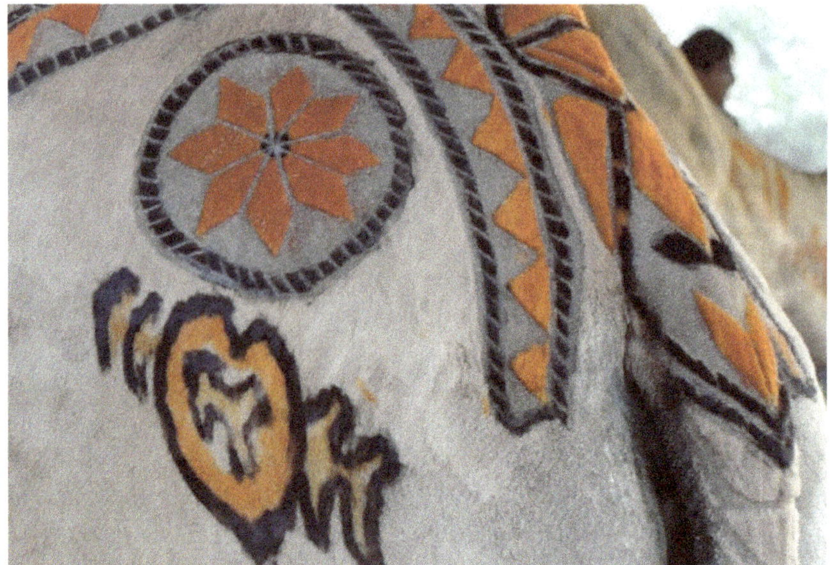

Source: Photograph by Muhammad Shafeeq, Channan Pir 2013.

As the weeks and months pass by and the hair grow longer, the motifs and symbols gradually lose their clarity and sharpness. In about six months there is hardly a trace of the motifs left on the camel's body.

Generally, the trained camels are selected for adornment to participate in the yearly traditional and spiritual activities. Indeed, the true picture of the beautiful hair cut artistry can be observed in the spiritual carnival at the shrine of the Sufi sage Channan Pir (figure 14). The artists residing in the interior of Cholistan practice the hair art of camels for their pleasure and spiritual satisfaction. Although the artists are underprivileged and live off modest means but still they do not demand much money from their patrons. The patrons also try to help by assisting them through the hair cutting process in whatever way possible.

Figure 14. Tattooed Camel on Channan Pir Festival

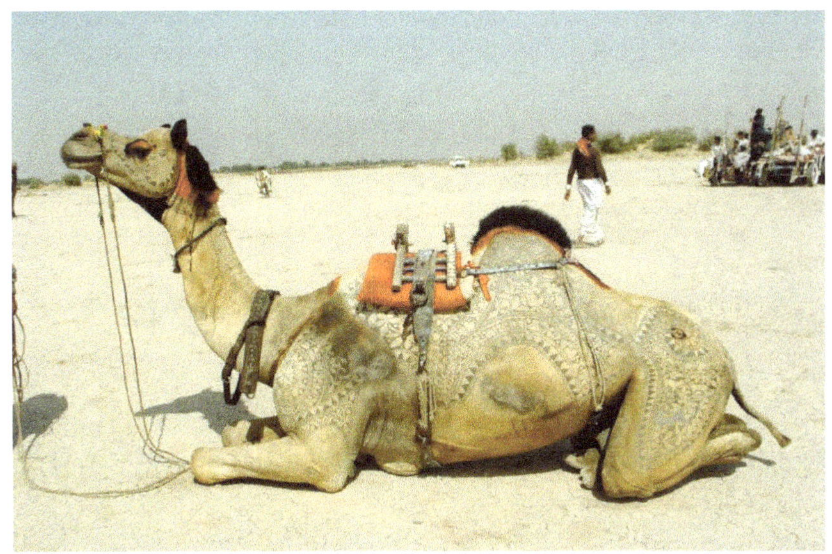

Source: Photograph by Muhammad Shafeeq, Channan Pir 2014.

The recorded history of Cholistan shows no traces of the art of camel hair tattoo. This book is an attempt to investigate the symbols and motifs of camel hair tattoo art which are particularly investigated with reference to the native religious beliefs, prominent Eastern and Western philosophical concepts and the historical accounts of Cholistan, Pakistan. Various distinguished and well-known artists of camel hair tattoo have been interviewed on various places in Cholistan. The notable artists namely Nazir Heer, Iqbal Dhaya, Jam Abdul Wahid, Muhammad Bukhsh Midan and Gul Muhammad have been specifically highlighted in the book due to their general recognition and contribution for promoting the fascinating art of camel hair tattoo. They have also been selected on the basis of different styles, techniques, cultural norms and ancestral leanings that each of them epitomizes.

This book is first of its kind to document the unique hair tattoo art, and to unravel its charm and beauty to a wider audience. The philosophic ideas behind this exuberant art have been analyzed with reference to some Eastern and Western philosophers. These philosophers have been quoted to develop a deeper understanding of camel hair tattoo art and its symbols rooted in the Islamic spirituality, traditions and cultures. Unfortunately, no historical record of camel hair tattoo could be found in the local literature. Therefore, the prime aim of this study is to preserve and enliven this beautiful art form. It will also open new avenues for further studies on other aspects of this mysterious and enchanting form of art.

CHAPTER 2

Historical Background

To study the art of camel hair tattoo with reference to its history reveals some very interesting missing links. The hidden nature of this art can perhaps be attributed to the fact that it has not been taken into any serious consideration by the native scholars of the subcontinent, let alone the study of meanings concerning its symbols, artistic heritage, philosophic and mystic affiliations.

This book is an effort to explore and understand the historical links of camel hair tattoo symbols and motifs used therein. In short, the artistic, geographical, cultural and the religious aspects are all summed up to unveil the hidden aspects of mystifying art of camel hair tattoo as practiced in Cholistan, Pakistan. Also, an attempt to decode the symbols and motifs of camel hair tattoo has been made to discover astonishing ancestral roots dating back to the prehistoric rock art in neighboring India. The motifs also have a strong resemblance with the pottery of Mehrgarh and Harappa. Local flora and cosmological symbolism are beautifully employed in this enchanting art form. Also the dimension of spiritual inspiration instils this art with a nameless beauty.

To begin with, we have to go deep in to the prehistoric times when man began to experiment with art. One of the most significant prehistoric art forms that survives to this day is rock art in the caves. More than 5000 centers of prehistoric cave murals have been discovered in India since 1880. These explorations of cave art in India mentioned in the book *Recent Perspectives on Prehistoric Art in India* include the rock art sites of Tarsang in Gujarat; Bhimbetka, Narsinghgarh, Naryaoli and North Raisen Region in Madhya Pradesh; and Sahibee River Valley in Rajasthan.[6] The rock art produced in these sites have images of animals with similar geometrical lines of camel hair tattoo. Most of these rock sites mark the border of Rajasthan state in India with adjoining Cholistan desert in Pakistan. The relationship of angles and movement of the geometrical lines painted within the bodies of these prehistoric mural animals indicate similar ancestral links with the art of camel hair tattoo in Cholistan. The

---

[6]. R.K. Sharma and K.K. Tripathi, ed. *Recent Perspectives on Prehistoric art in India* (New Delhi: Aryan Books International, 1996).

details of some of the prehistoric rock murals will be discussed in the chapter on the symbols and motifs of camel hair tattoo art.

It is pertinent to mention here that at the Mesolithic times, the domestication of camel coincides with the fifth phase of Bhimbetka caves marking the end of hunting phases of the cave man. At that transitional phase from hunting to agricultural life the Bhimbetka caves showed animal figures covered with geometrical lines resembling those used in camel hair tattoo (figure 15). It helps to understand the focus of the cave artist who painted multiple lines with red ochre color covering the entire body of the animal (figure 16). He may have tried to depict his emotional attachment with the animals by using red tones because his life at that time was dependent on animals. Similarly, the Ruhilas even till now place camels very high in their lives as their living relies heavily on camels. In fact, the use of intricate lineation, vegetal motifs and red *henna* dye on camel's body depicts their deep affection with the animal.

Figure 15. Camel Hair Tattoo Lineation

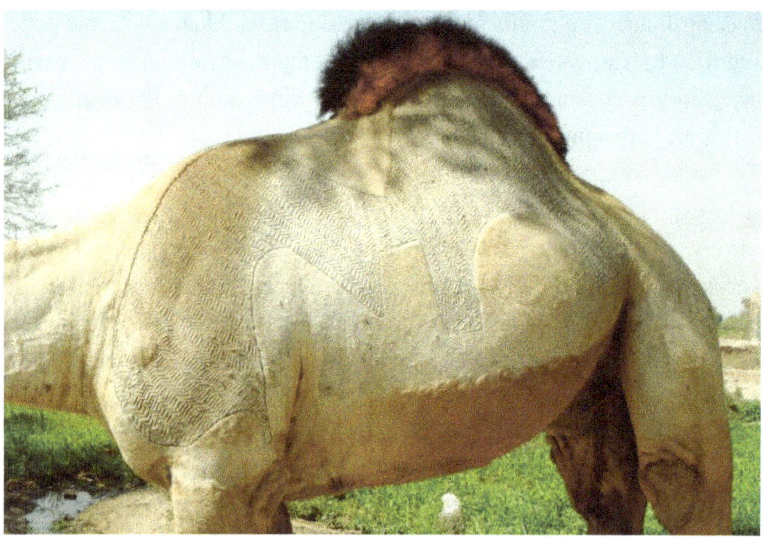

Source: Photograph by Muhammad Shafeeq, Miranian 2014.

Figure 16. Cave Paintings with Animals Figures

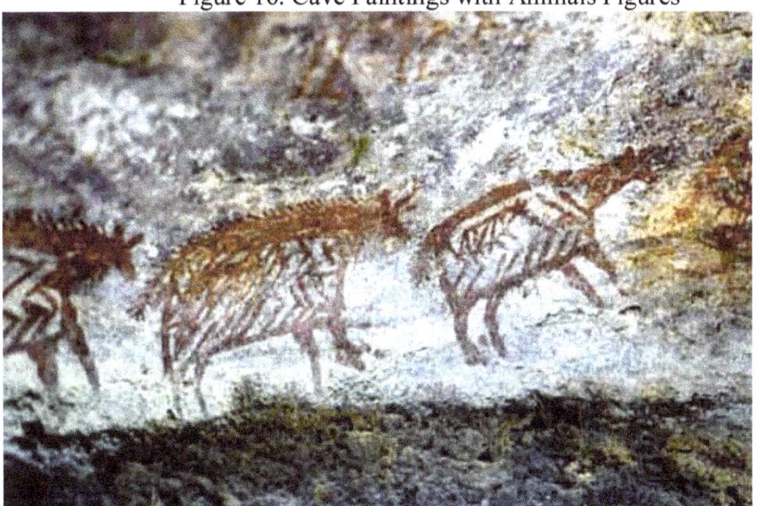

Source: Ram Chajja, District Raisen, Madhya Pradesh http://ignca.nic.in/asp/showbig.asp?projid=rock (accessed February 28, 2014).

The archaeologists have found model carts and dromedary-type camel figurines to observe that camels used to pull carts with food and other goods to Altyn Depe (a Bronze Age site in Turkmenistan inhabited in the 3rd to 2nd millennia B.C.) from near distances.[7] Similarly, Zaman Auj in his book, *Harappan Heritage* has mentioned that the recent excavations showed close contacts between Indus Valley and Bronze Age settlements in southern Turkmenia.[8]

The Indus Valley Civilization carried the similar motifs present in the ancient pottery of Mehrgarh in Balochistan, Pakistan around 6,500 years ago (figure 17). Astonishingly, the geometrical patterns of hair tattoo art have a remarkable resemblance with the designs found on the pottery of the Indus Valley Civilization of Harappa and Mohenjodaro in Pakistan belonging to the period about 5,000 years back (figure 18). The similarities include the zigzag, wavy and curved lines which were significantly in practice during the Indus Valley times are strikingly similar to the motifs of camel hair tattoo art.

---

7. George Erdosy, ed. *The Indo-Aryans of Ancient South Asia: Language, Material Cultural and Ethnicity* (Berlin: Walter de Gruyter, 1995), 208.

8. Nurul Zaman Ahmad Auj, *Harappan Heritage* (Multan: Caravan Book Centre, 1998), 7.

Figure 17. Indus Valley Pottery Vessel

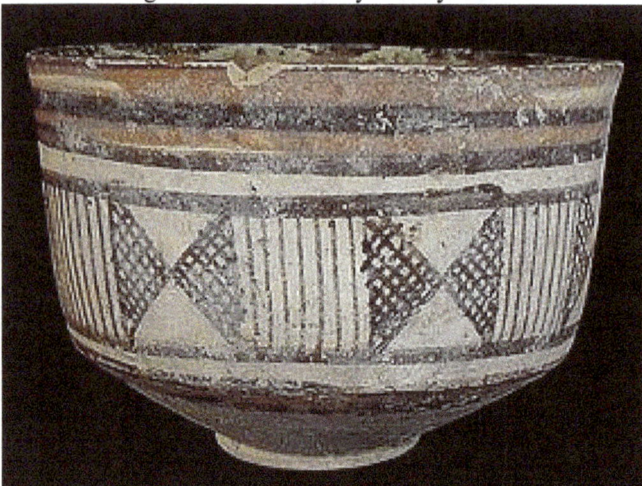

Source: Mehrgarh Culture, Balochistan. 3300-3000 B.C.
http://www.trocadero.com/stores/bcgalleries/items/1138230/item1138230.html (accessed February 11, 2013).
An Indus Valley painted buff ware cup with geometric design in brown pigment
Height: 80 mm, Diameter: 110 mm.

Figure 18. Indus Valley Terracotta Vessel

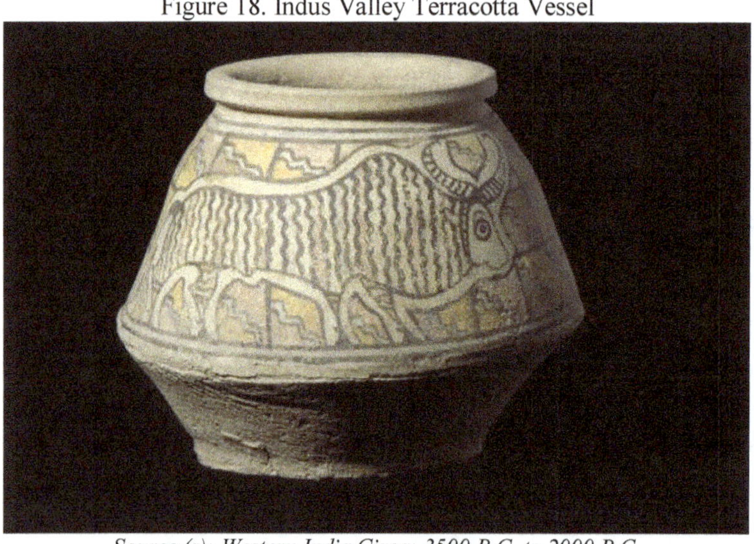

Source (s): Western India Circa: 3500 B.C. to 2000 B.C.
http://www.antiques.com/classified/Antiquities/Ancient-Near-East/Antique-Indus-Valley-Terracotta-Vessel---LO-1287 (accessed January 27, 2015).
An Indus Valley terracotta large painted pot with geometric and animal motifs
Height: 15. 5 cm, Diameter: 7. 50 cm.

Interestingly, one often comes across cows and bulls in present day Cholistan that bear henna marks in the various tree-like motifs and geometrical patterns of crosses, circles and stars all resembling the animal motifs painted on the ancient vessels found in Harappa and Mehrgarh (figure 19 & 20).

Figure 19. Tree like Henna Dye Motifs

Source: Photograph by Muhammad Shafeeq, Channan Pir, Cholistan. 2014.
The tree- like motif painted on the neck with henna dye resemble the motifs on the Indus Valley terra-cotta pot.

Figure 20. Indus Valley Terracotta Large Pot

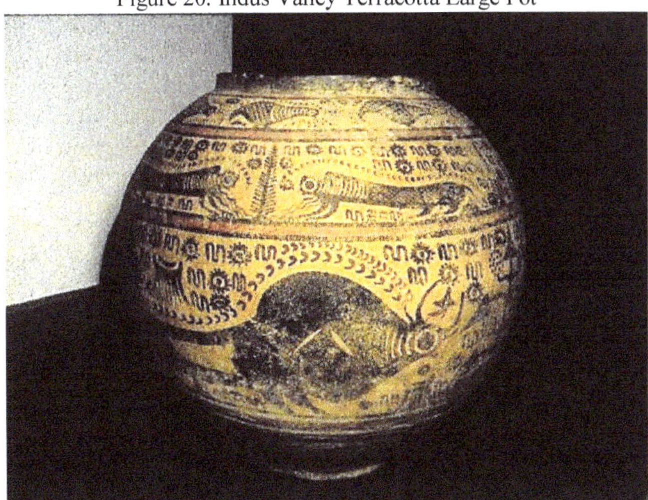

Source: Mehrgarh Culture, Balochistan. 2500-2000 BCE
http://www.jgalleries.com/index.php?route=product/product&product_id=199 (accessed January 27, 2015).
A Mehrgarh terracotta large painted pot with geometric designs and tree like motifs
Height: 32 cm, Diameter: 24cm.

In Cholistan, every tribe has its own distinct totem mark which is in fact a permanent mark of a metal stamp. This metal stamp is put on fire and then stamped on a hind quarter of the camels. This painful process leaves the permanent totem mark on the camel's body and is used to identify as to which tribe a camel belongs to. These totems have a remarkable similarity with the curved and tree-like motifs which strongly point to the ancestral links with the art of Indus Valley (figure 21). These simple desert dwellers who are mostly illiterate and are largely isolated from the rest of the world but their totems and camel hair tattoo motifs mark great similarities. It points to the sole reason that these tribesmen are the remnants of the Indus Valley Civilization who are intuitively carrying their artistic and cultural traditions uninterruptedly. The American art historian Roy C. Craven (1924–1996) mentioned that in the third millennium B.C. before the advent of the Harappan culture the aborigines of India worshipped spirits of trees, waters, serpents and earth with some spirits having human forms.[9] Still, some traces of worshipping such elements can be found in Uch which is located at the periphery of Cholistan desert. The motifs of trees in camel hair tattoo may also have been the result of the ancient influences of these sacred practices.

Figure 21. Indus Valley Terracotta Large Pot

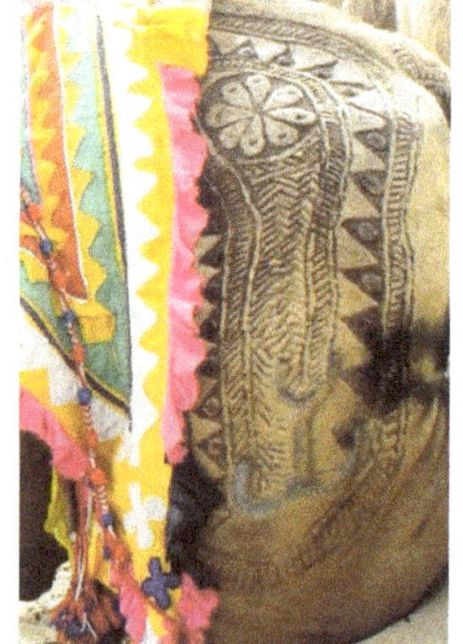

Source: Photograph by Muhammad Shafeeq, Channan Pir, Cholistan. 2014.
The tree like totem mark similar to Indus Valley terracotta's tree motif.

---

[9]. Roy C. Craven, *Indian Art: A Concise History* (London: Thames and Hudson, 2001), 45.

Muhammad Rafique Mughal (b. 1936), the most prominent Pakistani archaeologist, argued in his book *Ancient Cholistan: Archaeology and Architecture* that the art of pottery making can be considered as the most ancient art of Cholistan. It was discovered along the dried bed of Hakra River and was named as the Hakra wares (3500 -3000 B.C.). The distinct patterns of the Hakra wares that were stamped on the outer surface were discovered in 1941 by the Hungarian born British explorer and archaeologist, Sir Aurel Stein (1862–1943) who once also served as the registrar of the University of the Punjab, Lahore, Pakistan. He described them, "with shreds decorated with impressed patterns". These artefacts were in fact, the Painted Grey Wares. Their impressed geometrical designs of triangles and circles bear almost the same impressions like that of the camel hair tattoo art. It strongly suggests that the people of Cholistan were fond of using these geometrical findings in their arts and crafts for the past centuries.[10]

The people of Indus Valley established the basis of Indian concepts of cosmology and the structure of calendar. They divided the year in three large and six small seasons. The small seasons were depicted by animals like unicorn, bull, tiger and goat. While the zoomorphic symbols meant the long seasons, for example, the crocodile represented the flooding of rivers. The sixty year cycle named as the cycle of Jupiter was also the contribution of the Harappans which later led the Aryans to divide this cycle into five twelve-year periods.[11] It is important to mention here that in camel hair tattoo art we find the similar traces of the divisions of circles probably to depict the cycle of seasons and the cosmos. The floral motifs have petals ranging from five to eight often depicted in the center probably to denote the seasons. Whereas, the triangular bands surrounding the floral motifs could perhaps be depicting the cosmic star movements. The figure shows floral pattern with six petals depicted on the shoulder blade of the camel (figure 22). The floral motif is surrounded by a band having twelve triangles which may symbolize the universe having star cycles of the cosmos rooted in the cosmogony concepts of the Harappans.

---

[10]. Muhammad Rafique Mughal, *Ancient Cholistan: Archaeology and Architecture* (Lahore: Ferozsons, 1997), 35.

[11]. Ibid., 9.

Figure 22. Floral Motif encircled by the Triangular Band

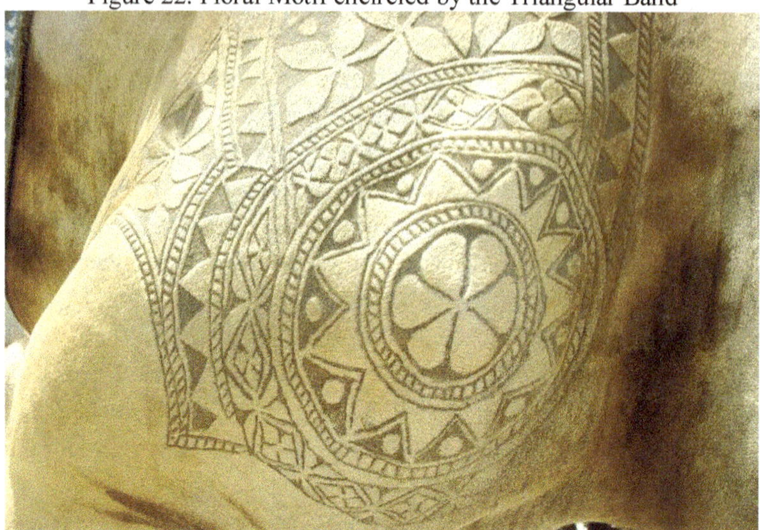

Source: Photograph by Muhammad Shafeeq, Ahmad Pur, Cholistan 2014

The Floral motif encircled with twelve triangles in the triangular band show cosmic movements.

Nurul Zaman Auj has quoted the Finnish artist on South Asian Studies, Asko Parpola (b. 1941), who observed that in Sumerian seals the picture of star represented the goddess Ishtar, which is the same word as Esther of the Old Testament. Greek 'aster' and Persian 'akhtar' meaning star which has been derived from the same Sumerian word Ishtar. The word 'star' occurs frequently in Sumerian texts since deciphered. Parpola adds that the significant symbol of the 'fish' is called 'min' and is used as a 'star' in the Dravidian language. Therefore, the Indus seal having the symbol of fish may symbolize an astronomical myth.[12] So far no fish motif has been observed on camels but the symbol of star is frequently used by all the artists of camel hair tattoo regardless of their tribes. The Balochi tribals prefer to depict four or six pointed star on the hump of the camel while the typical Saraiki tribals appreciate five pointed star which they claim to have been derived from the flag of Pakistan. Interestingly, the six pointed star (also called the Star of David) is also prominent on dilapidated ruins of the popular tomb of Bibi Jawindi in Uch.

The Vedas of the Aryans written between 1500 and 500 B.C. mentioned the supremacy of their gods and their power with reference to many elements of

---

[12]. Nurul Zaman Ahmad Auj, *Harappan Heritage* (Multan: Caravan Book Centre, 1998), 19-20.

nature. Camel is also mentioned five times in different hymns of the Vedas. It showed that at that time the people for whom these scriptures were written were aware of the camel. In the Yajur Veda of Aryans under the, "Prapathaka 6: The Piling of the Fire Altar, Mantra no. 21: The Pairs of Victims," the camel has been discussed as a symbol of power. It goes:

> To Soma, self-ruler, there are (to be offered) two oxen which drag the cart; to Indra and Agni, the givers of force, two camels; to Indra and Agni, givers of might.[13]

The Ruhilas have originated from the native race of Dravidians which faced constant invasions of Aryans, then Jats, Balochis and later Iranians. Still, they seem to maintain their centuries old traditions.[14] The Aryans first came to the Indus Valley and later shifted to the Ganges River Valley. They brought with them the horses and the skill to make iron tools and implements. These Aryans had oral traditions and learnt the writing skills from the ancient Harappans.[15]

The hostile climate and hard living conditions of Cholistan did not suit the invaders including the Aryans though some settlements survived because of the fact that the dried bed of Hakra River was converted into a route passing from Sindh and Uch towards northern India.[16] Thus, the links between Cholistan and the other significant centers of art in India were established. It shows that the camel as the beast of burden was used to travel frequently between all the major cities in the subcontinent for the trading of goods.

Here, to the focus the study on camel hair tattoo art we must discuss the origin of camels in the subcontinent. To begin with, we find the most influential Greek philosopher, Aristotle (384–322 BC) whose seminal work on the historical advances of animals compiled in his book titled, *History of Animals* wrote that the two species of camels are differentiated by one and two humps namely Bactrian and the Arabian. The Bactrian camel has two humps and the Arabian has one.[17] Similarly, in his book titled *Studies in Ancient Technology* the author R.J. Forbes

---

[13]. "The Vedas: An English-only, Indexed Version of the 4 Veda Smahitas in One Document," https://zelalemkibret.files.wordpress.com/2012/03/the-4-vedas.pdf (accessed January 27, 2015).

[14]. Nurul Zaman Ahmad Auj, *Harappan Heritage* (Multan: Caravan Book Centre, 1998), 74.

[15]. Ibid., 8.

[16]. Ibid., 75.

[17]. Wentworth Thompson, trans. *History of Animals,* http://pinkmonkey.com/dl/library1/gp007.pdf (accessed July 18, 2014).

(1900–1973) argued in the chapter titled, "The Coming of Camels" that the dromedary camels (camelus dromedarius) are the one-humped Arabian camels while the other one with two humps named Bactrian camel helped to establish links across the desert. The dromedaries appear to be most useful animals for the desert dwellers of Arabia. The Arabs used their milk, meat, wool, dung and skin calling them the "milk giving palm of the animals." The author quoted about dromedaries that Allah blessed the Muslims with the camel and its milk and despised the Christians. He argued that the prehistoric wild form of the dromedary (Camelus Thomasi Pom) probably retreated into desert regions before the wetter climate of the Later Palaeolithic. Agatarchides claimed that in his days there still were wild dromedaries in Arabia and they may still be there now. This was the wild form tamed by the desert-dwellers and used as a riding animal long before the introduction of the horse in these regions.[18]

Forbes claimed that Persia was famous for its camels and camel breeders.[19] Furthermore, the dromedaries in Persian times had been used for military purposes and have travelled to the Persian desert for trade with India along the southern route. Significantly, the dromedaries were present in Arabia from early the Neolithic times and its domestication began in the Mesolithic times when man was passing from hunting to the agricultural phases.[20]

On the eve of Christianity, the Northern India followed a series of important changes in art and culture. The significant trade routes were established between Rome and Asia and also across the great Silk Route. The trade systems spanned from Western China through Persia and the Levant to the shores of Mediterranean. Also, the other connecting routes started from the high plateaus of Central Asia passing through the Himalayan Mountains to the plains of India. When the Parthians became closely connected with the Rome the older trade with the Levant was no longer in practice. Therefore, the highways through the Indian mountain passes were established for the camel caravans.[21] The art of Parthians depicted some two humped Bactrian camels carved in the stone reliefs of that era. But there are no patterns and motifs found on their bodies.

By the middle of the third century, the East and the West trade links were interrupted due to the fact that the Sassanians defeated the Parthians of Persia and captured Taxila and Peshawar weakening the Kushan Empire. Still Buddhism

---

[18]. R.J. Forbes *Studies in Ancient Technology* (Leiden: Library of Congress, 1965), 194.

[19]. Ibid., 195.

[20]. Ibid., 196.

[21]. Roy C. Craven, *Indian Art: A Concise History* (London: Thames and Hudson, 2001), 81-82.

continued to exist in Gandhara at least into the eighth century. At that time, the Buddhists had to move from their places and built their monasteries along the trade route joining Taxila and Bactria. The paintings and sculptures of that time showed a blend of Indian and Iranian styles. Significantly, the grottoes of Bamiyan in Afghanistan are remarkable for their paintings including the motifs adapted from the Sassanian fabric designs. Also, the colossal statues of Buddha carved in the cliffs there showed Hindu influences including the images of Hindu sun god, Surya. It depicts cosmological influences including the mandala form to highlight the mysterious aspects of Buddhism.[22] Also, the circular patterning of camel hair tattoo art have similarities with the patterns of circles of Buddhist Art in the Ajanta Caves. It shows influences of Buddhist cosmological symbols in the camel hair tattoo art of Cholistan.

Geographically, Cholistan extends from Sutlej then along the left bank of Indus up to the border of Sind. It was once a fertile land irrigated by Hakra or Ghaggar River, also known as Sarasvati in Vedas. An interesting analysis of various viewpoints about the Hakra River has been proposed by the Pakistani researchers of Pakistan Studies, Samia Khalid and Aftab Hussain Gilani in their paper, "Distinctive Cultural and Geographical Legacy of Bahawalpur" that:

> [Hakra River] was the southern tributary of Sutlej River… but to some others, it was a separate river system in itself, which used to fall in the Gulf of the Rann of Kutch and some considered it the upper part of the Nara River of Sindh. However, all are unanimous about its extinction. There is another opinion that its neighboring river Jumna, which springs from its source near Himalayas, it is also called Saraswati with its Vedic name apart from Hakra, Ghaghra or Ghaghar. Even today it enters Indian Territory of Bekaneer as a rearing stream and sometimes its water also enters Bahawalpur.[23]

It is interesting to note here that Bikaner was a very old and important center of the Indian desert and has been notably mentioned by various scholars and historians. Nurul Zaman Auj quoted Charles Masson (1800–1853) in his book, *Harappan Heritage* that:

---

22. Ibid., 97-98.

23. Samia Khalid and Aftab Ḥussain Gilani, "Distinctive Cultural and Geographical Legacy of Bahawalpur," *Pakistaniaat: A Journal of Pakistan Studies*, no. 2, (2010), 13, http://pakistaniaat.org/index.php/pak/article/download/62/62 (accessed February 25, 2015).

> The portion of desert stretching eastward of Bahawalpur to Bikaneer is of course but little productive, yet, as in many parts of it, the surface has more soil than sand... In this tract also, the camel thrives exceedingly, and finds ample sustenance in the prickly and saline plants which cover the surface... In remote times, rivers flowed through and fertilized this now sterile country; their beds may in many places be traced; and numerous vestiges remain of ancient towns in burned bricks and fragments strewed in the soil.[24]

Significantly, the desert of Cholistan is rich in artistic and cultural heritage of Indus Valley and possess numerous ancient artefacts buried under its sand. Interestingly, during the expedition to Cholistan to find the artists of camel hair tattoo, various terra-cotta pieces of pottery were seen lying neglected on the sands of Derawar village, Kalay Par and Ganeriwala showing large number of ancient terra-cotta pottery pieces.

In addition, Nurul Zaman Auj has described in *Harappan Heritage* that Cholistan was one of the earliest places in the subcontinent to receive Muslim saints including Shaikh Saif ud-Din Ghazruni who came from Baghdad in 980 A.D. and settled in Uch, Cholistan. He founded the earliest Darul Alum of Islamic learning named as Firuzi University to develop Uch as the seat of Islamic learning. Uch was strategically a significant place as it was then situated at the confluence of the Indus and Chenab rivers. Now this point of confluence has moved a hundred kilometers away at Mithankut.

It is significant to mention here that some traces of sun temples have been found in the historical city of Uch. One of the most significant temples was in Muhallah Khawajgan of Uch where the family of Haji Sharif is currently residing. His sons Abdul Razzaq and Muhammad Jamil claimed that at the place of their house once there was a sun temple where a lamp was lighted in a niche for worshipping. The Sun temple was completely demolished at the time they constructed their home after the local Hindus had migrated to India at the time of the partition in 1947. Abdul Razzaq claimed that the Sun temple had four pillars on four sides that their father Haji Sharif had witnessed himself. Its interior used to be full of floral and geometrical motifs and had no figure statue or painting for worshipping. Instead, the light of lamp was worshipped as a symbol of God.[25] This could have been due to Iranian invasion of the region that brought Zoroastrian religion to the place.

---

[24]. Nurul Zaman Ahmad Auj, *Harappan Heritage* (Multan: Caravan Book Centre, 1998), 73-74.

[25]. Abdul Razzaq and Muhammad Jamil in discussion with the author, November 2013.

No trace of the other two Hindu temples could be found as they had been completely demolished and encroached upon. An old folk of Uch named Allah Ditta disclosed that they were once in Muhallah Bawli presently called Muhallah Bukhari after the name of native Sufi Sayyid Jalal Surkh Bukhari. One temple had statues of Hindu gods resembling human figures for worshipping and the other had a *pipal* (ficus religiosa) tree which was worshipped by the Hindus. Allah Ditta added that Sun, Moon, Cow, River, Tree, Fire were also worshipped in Uch. He further claimed that at the house of Haji Sharif, previously discussed, had a temple where fire was worshipped and the Hindu priest used to gather children around the fire proclaiming "Ram Ram" (the name of a Hindu god). The fire was lighted with *harmal* (peganum harmala) seeds and *phatkari* (alum).[26]

Significantly, some other sources concerning ancient Indian mysticism, art and culture have been traced. Notably, a Classical Greek physician, Ctesias who served as a court physician to Artaxerxes II Mnemon, the king of Persia wrote in fifth century B.C. a book on the stories of India titled *Indica.* As a court physician he had access to the traders who use to travel from Persia to India along the silk route. Based on the accounts of traders he wrote mythical things about Indian land and people. He mentioned a sacred place in the Indian desert, falconry, variety of oils, expensive metals, domesticated animals, palm trees, integrity and morality of the Indians, and their ideal life and health.[27] The British Orientalist Horace Hayman Wilson (1786–1860), in his book, *Notes on the Indica of Ctesias,* quoted Ctesias as follows:

> There is no rain, and that the lands are watered by the inundations of the rivers; that there is neither thunder nor lightning, but frequent gales and hurricanes. The heat is so great, that in summer many are suffocated by it, and the Sun seems to be twice as large as in other parts of the world. The rising sun diffuses coolness, and for thirty five days in the year, at a certain place which is sacred to the Sun and the Moon, situated in an almost inaccessible tract, at a distance of fifteen days' journey from the mountains

---

[26]. Allah Ditta (a native of Uch) in discussion with the author, November 2013.

[27]. J. M. Bigwood, *Ctesias' Indica and Photius,* http://www.electronicsandbooks.com/eab1/manual/Magazine/P/Phoenix%20CA/1989/Bigwood%20-%201989%20-%20Ctesias'%20Indica%20and%20Photius.pdf (accessed March, 7, 2015).

> that yield the sardonyx, the Sun restrains his rays on purpose that pilgrims coming to an annual festival held there may not be burnt alive.[28]

Wilson explained the words of Ctesias claiming that:

> A tract of between four and five hundred miles in length, and about two hundred in breath, on the east of the valley of the Indus, is known to the Hindus as the *maru desa*, the dry country or desert; being for the most part an arid waste, thinly sprinkled with spots of cultivation, the miserable inhabitants of which, according to Col. Tod, calculate upon a partial famine every third year...the Indian deserts of Jeselmer and Parkur.[29]

Wilson also quoted from *Indica* that this festival was held in the Indian desert in the moderate season that lasted for thirty five days. Interestingly, the yearly Channan Pir festival of Cholistan continues for five weeks in the days of spring when the Sun is not so hot. It is probable that this festival is a continuation of that same historical festival though draped in Islamic colors. During the course of history, different religious beliefs emerged and vanished but the mystical and cultural practices of the Cholistan desert have retained their identity in some way.

After the advent of Islam, the Arabian camel spread across the parts of the subcontinent. Also, the Dutch professor of South Asian History, Jos Gommans (b. 1963) has mentioned camels in his book *Mughal Warfare* that in South Asia the spread of the one humped camel has been the result of the expansion of Islam after 1000 A.D. Later, the Indian breeds of dromedaries have been developed in Balochistan and Rajasthan. During the Mughal Era the cross breeding of one humped female dromedaries with the two-humped male Bactrian camels have been accomplished for stronger breeds. Significantly, the reign of Mughal Emperor Akbar (1542–1605) who ruled the subcontinent from 1556 until his death, has been considered ideal for camel breeding used in wars and trade. He had 6 to 7,000 camels in his army. Significantly, the North-Western Indian region of the Thar Desert of Rajasthan has been famous for producing excellent camel breeds. The Balochi and Raibari nomads have also been known for their high quality camel breeds that were hired for warfare by the Mughal Emperor Akbar. The Balochi tribes also played significant role in breeding and transporting

---

[28]. Horace Hayman Wilson, *Notes on the Indica of* Ctesias, (Collingwood: Collingwood printing, 1836), 14–15.

[29]. Ibid., 15.

camels to Daira Ismail Khan, Daira Fateh Khan and Daira Ghazi Khan of the central Indus Valley during the late fifteenth century. Abul Fazl (1551-1602), the vizier of the Emperor Akbar mentioned the dromedary breeding and training skills of the Hindu Raibari tribe of Rajasthan which helped them to cover long distances in a short time.[30] But the historical evidences of Muslim miniature paintings, pottery and architectural mural paintings of that time show no traces of camel hair tattoo art. It might have been possible that the camels used at that time were only decorated with the textiles and ornaments without much need for hair cutting. Even if the art of camel hair tattoo was present at that time it might have been centered only in some isolated areas of Cholistan and Rajasthan deserts.

Nurul Zaman Auj has described in *Harappan Heritage* the Muslim rulers who have been very influential in spreading the Islamic influences in the desert of Cholistan. He argued that in the early 17th century, Daudputra Abbasi founded the State of Bahawalpur at Derawar, Cholistan. During the two hundred years rule of the Abbasi dynasty the Islamic traditions were enforced in Cholistan. They also saved the culture of Cholistan from the Sikhs, the Jats of Bharatpur and the Nawab of Oudh but they enjoyed good relations with Marhattas, British and Afghan invaders.[31]

The art and architecture of the subcontinent has been influenced by the Muslims including Arabs, Persians, Turks and later the Mughals. The Muslim art and architecture comprised of calligraphy composed with various vegetal and geometrical motifs. It is important to mention here that the Muslims consciously avoided the use of animated imagery and explored the mystical dimensions of geometry significantly observed in their architecture. Following the traditions, the Abbasi Nawabs of Bahawalpur played very important role for the development of architecture in Cholistan. They laid the foundations of numerous forts in Cholistan witnessing the glory of Muslim art and architecture. These significantly include the forts namely Derawar, Moj Garh, Meer Garh, Jam Garh, Khan Garh and Khair Garh etc. The Abbasis were great patrons of art including the fascinating camel hair tattoo art. Abdul Kareem, the resident of a village opposite to Derawar Fort, claimed that his forefathers were camel hair tattoo artists and were patronized by the Abbasi lords. The Abbasis, he informed, liked hair

---

[30]. Jos Gommans, *Mughal Warfare: Indian Frontiers and High Roads to Empire* 1500-1700 (London: Routledge, 2002), 126-127.

[31]. Nurul Zaman Ahmad Auj, *Harappan Heritage* (Multan: Caravan Book Centre, 1998), 76.

tattooed camels for riding and travelling in the desert. He added that the art of camel hair tattoo is much older than the Abbasis in the Cholistan region.[32]

Also, Auj has quoted David Ross who wrote about Cholistan that:

> The desert portion of Bahawalpur has been very little explored, and it is believed that there are many ancient ruins along the old bed of rivers which flowed through this territory, either covered by the ridges or hillocks several hundred feet in height.[33]

Significantly, Cholistan has contributed well to the fields of history and literature. The first history of Sindh, *Chachnamah*, was written at Uch. The notable Sufi poet Khawaja Farid (1845-1901) is considered the greatest poet of Cholistan. He strongly influenced the people of Cholistan through his mystical poetry. [34]

One of the most well-known Sufi saints named Channan Pir was born with mystic qualities in Cholistan. According to the folklore his father was a Hindu named Raja Sadharan who saw in a dream that his child to be born will be a Muslim therefore, when Channan Pir were born, his father ordered his son to be killed but suddenly the cradle of Channan Pir ascended to heaven and the mystic child was saved. Later, the Sufi Channan Pir became the disciple of Makhdum Jahaniyan Jahangasht (1308–1384) of Uch.[35] The tomb of the Sufi is about sixty five kilometers from Bahawalpur City. Every year thousands of devotees visit Channan Pir for seven consecutive Thursdays beginning from March to April.

The Scottish traveler, author, painter and filmmaker Elizabeth Balneaves (1911–2006) has mentioned Channan Pir festival in her book, *The Waterless Moon.* She goes:

> Out in the lonely desert areas of Bahawalpur and Cholistan there still remains an undercurrent of the primitive and the barbaric. To the flat tinkle of the *ghangroos* or camel bells the nomadic desert tribes, their women and children perched high in great panniers on the camels.[36]

Khalid and Gilani in their paper, "Distinctive Cultural and Geographical Legacy of Bahawalpur," wrote about the State of Bahawalpur that it was founded by Nawab Sadiq Muhammad Khan Abbasi in 1739. The first English book on the State of Bahawalpur published in the mid 19th century says:

---

32. Abdul Kareem (camel hair tattoo artist) in discussion with the author, November 2013.

33. Ibid., 72.

34. Ibid., 217.

35. Ibid., 218.

36. Ibid., 221.

> This state was bounded on the east by the British possession of Sirsa, and on the west by the river Indus; the river Garra forms its northern boundary, Bikaner and Jeyselmeer are on its southern frontier... its length from east to west was 216 koss or 324 English miles. Its breadth varies much: in some parts it is eighty, and in other from sixty to fifteen miles.[37]

The natives of Bahawalpur are generally Saraiki speaking people. They belong to different castes and thus have many dialects including Multani, Jhangi, Sindhi and Thali.[38] They include the notable mystics namely Shaikh Saif ud-din Haqqani and Pir Jalal ud-din Qutab-al-Aqtab (died in 1292). In the early thirteenth century four significant Sufis popular as *char yar*, meaning four friends, included Hazrat Sayyid Jalal ud-din Bukhari (1196-1294) of Uch and Hazrat Bahaud-din Zakariyah of Multan (1170–1267). The Sufi shrines in Uch are of the Ṣufis Hazrat Sayyid Jalal ud-din Surkh Bukhari (1199–1291), Hazrat Bahawal Halim, Hazrat Sayyid Jalal ud-din Bukhari popular as Makhdum Jahanian Jahangasht (1307–1383), and Bibi Jind-waddi popular as Bibi Jawandi (died c. 1492) and Shaikh Saif ud-din Ghazruni.[39] The shrines of the saints in Uch are beautifully adorned with glazed tiles having remarkable symbols of stars, flora and calligraphic verses from the Holy Quran.

The prominent Sufi mystic poet of the area, Khawaja Farid meditated in the deep desert of Cholistan. Christopher Shackle (b. 1942), mentioned about the mystical dimensions of the Sufi poetry of Khawaja Farid as:

> Only in the hands of Khawaja Ghulam Farid of Bahawalpur does the long tradition of Islamic mystical poetry in the Indus Valley blaze into a fine splendor, an all-embracing poetic language which can perhaps emerge only once in the history of a given literature. The rainbow certainly continues to glitter in the sky and the lines of camels do cross the dunes in the pages of his successors, who find themselves his helpless imitators. But for all their reiteration of the sweetness of sounds of cattle-bells or drizzling rain, that rich or elusive message magic which is the hallmark of Khawaja Farid's style can no longer exert the same

---

[37]. Samia Khalid and Aftab Ḥussain Gilani, "Distinctive Cultural and Geographical Legacy of Bahawalpur," *Pakistaniaat: A Journal of Pakistan Studies*, no. 2 (2010): 13, http://pakistaniaat.org/index.php/pak/article/download/62/62 (accessed February 25, 2015).
[38]. Ibid., 7.
[39]. Ibid., 8.

> spell. No one has composed more beautiful mystical poetry than he did.[40]

The Ruhilas of Cholistan spend their energies and resources to decorate their camels for the Sufi festivals. They move with their highly ornamented camels without much interest in their own apparels to gather at the shrine of their beloved Sufi to charge their spirits. They take along their hair tattooed camels as a gesture of their devotion to their Sufi. Much similar to Khawaja's Sufi poetry, an adorned tattooed camel symbolizes a true picture of Cholistan's natural beauty and spirit. The mystical symbols of camel hair tattoo can also be declared the pictorial version of Khawaja Farid's enchanting poetry. Thus, the art of camel hair tattoo has been nurtured in the ambit of esoteric Sufi creed which is a strong reason for its absence in the historical annals.

---

[40]. Nurul Zaman Ahmad Auj, *Harappan Heritage* (Multan: Caravan Book Centre, 1998), 269.

CHAPTER 3

The Distinct Artists of Camel Hair Tattoo Art

The venture to write this book took the author miles into the heart of the Cholistan desert. Finding the camel hair tattoo artists of Cholistan required intense efforts. There were no signboards, no paved roads, no adequate mobile phone communication service and not even a soul there for miles and miles to guide you. Going deep inside the desert, locating and interviewing the artists without fully knowing their language needed great courage, resilience and nerves. To top it all, being a female in an area that is still primitive in many respects was the greatest of all the handicaps. The natives also were non-cooperative in guiding about their fellow camel hair tattoo artists fearing the author to be some undercover government official collecting fines and taxes. These naive desert dwellers, who live in isolation, are perhaps still mentally haunted by their past when the government officials forcefully collected taxes from the poor subjects.

These desert dwellers of Cholistan, called the Ruhilas, are badly neglected by the government and are deprived of quality education, healthcare and clean drinking water. Ironically, the ancestors of these Ruhilas of Cholistan who are the descendants of the great Indus Valley Civilization once enjoyed the "water control [system] with a plethora of hydraulic features such as drains, wells, pits and baths"41 thousands of years back.

Here, in this chapter we will discuss the subject choices, styles and techniques of the camel hair tattoo artists with respect to their native areas in Cholistan. The centers of camel hair tattoo art that were explored by the author included Bahawalpur City, Ahmed Pur, Miranian, Derawar Fort, Latan Haar Shinghaar, Moj Garh Fort, Marut, Kalay Par, Khatri Bangla, Uch and Channan Pir. In the journey to explore this little known art the author met more than thirty hair tattoo artists of diverse styles and expressions. Only three notable artists namely Nazir Heer of Ahmad Pur, Iqbal Dhaya belonging to Derawar Fort village

[41]. Atta ur Rehman, Fawad Khan, Marcus Moench, Sharmeen Malik, Lea Sabbag & Karen Mac Clune, "Desk Study: Indus Floods Research," a Project by International Development Research Centre
http://r4d.dfid.gov.uk/pdf/outputs/CRISSA/Indus_Floods_Research_Appendix_5.pdf
(accessed May 12, 2013)

and Gul Muhammad who resides in the village opposite to Moj Garh Fort, have been selected for detailed analysis considering their general recognition. Their mastery over the art was also evident in their distinct styles and techniques, and their discourse. During interviews they all disclosed themselves as mystical aestheticians of camel hair tattoo art.

Bahawalpur City

The most easily accessible camel hair tattoo art center located on the periphery of Bahawalpur City is Chak 11 opposite the Bahawalpur Airport. There the brothers named Nazar Hussain and Khadim Hussain and their cousin Navid Hussain and Muhammad Habib live together in a large compound. They rear camels for milking, transporting, racing, dancing and hair tattooing. They learnt the basics of camel hair tattoo art from their family elder Muhammad Ramzan Gujjar, who himself was a renowned master but no longer practiced the art due to old age. These four men do not practice the art themselves but are great enthusiasts and patrons of the art. Ever since Muhammad Ramzan Gujjar relinquished camel hair tattooing a few years ago, they have been hiring the services of Nazir Heer, the renowned camel tattoo artist of Ahmad Pur East. Every year, the artist visits them for tattooing to adorn their camel for the annual festival at Channan Pir's Sufi shrine.

Close to Chak 11 is Chak 13, where another patron of camel hair tattoo art named Muhammad Javaid resides. He is an astute camel rider and like his friend Muhammad Habib of Chak 11 mentioned earlier, he also embellishes his camel with hair tattoo artistry for the holy festival of Sufi Channan Pir. In the year 2014 his camel caught some infection during the severe winter season and was unable to participate in racing and dancing activities. Muhammad Javaid informed the author with a tinge of sadness that he bought the camel for Pakistani rupees 350,000 with the savings of his lifetime but still could not tell if the camel would survive. He was serving the camel with local medicines and nutrients like almonds to save the camel's life.[42]

The Artist Nazir Heer of Ahmad Pur

Muhammad Javaid helped to reach Nazir Heer by giving his contact. The artist Nazir Heer was discovered tattooing the fur coat of a camel at the residence of his neighbor and old friend, Muhammad Ramzan, at Mozah Faizwa on Uch Road

---

[42]. Muhammad Javaid (camel hair tattoo artist) in discussion with the author, February 2014.

near Ahmad Pur. Nazir Heer was an uneducated down-to-earth man in his early fifties. For him camel hair tattooing is a passion.

Heer always begins camel hair tattoo art with his friend's camels at the beginning of spring season every year. Nazir Heer and Muhammad Ramzan had an association of more than fifty years. The reason to select Nazir Heer as a subject of this study is his exquisite hair cutting technique and style which is unparalleled among his contemporaries. He employs organic symbols and motifs which disclosed the hidden norms of his hair tattoo artistry.

As mentioned earlier, hair tattooing of a camel continues for several days. Nazir Heer claimed to take about five days to complete hair artistry of a camel with the help of his assistant. He disclosed in the interview that at the early age of 12 his father, who was also a well-known artist, saw his hair art talent and took him for formal training to a distinguished master of that time, Kattu Kalar (late) of Faizpur. Kattu Kalar trained Heer for three years in the complex hair cutting technique of the camel and also inculcated in him the true spirit of the art. Heer claimed that he realized much later as to why his father had not wanted him to get training at home from himself. He explained that his father had wanted him to undergo rigorous training from a distinguished master and that as a father he himself could not subject his son to such rigors. Heer informed that his father advised him to consider his teacher like a spiritual mentor and give more respect to him than a father.

Heer argued that it was indeed very hard to achieve mastery over cutting the coarse hair of the camel and only Ruhilas had been endowed with the blessing of camel's hair tattoo art. Heer pointed out that the ideal age of a camel for hair tattooing is around four years and a trained camel in dancing and racing bears the price of more than three hundred thousand Pakistani rupees. Also, the race camels are considered more valuable as compare to the other untrained camels and thus are not used for ordinary jobs of carrying loads.[43]

THE DISTINCTIVE TECHNIQUE OF NAZIR HEER

Nazir Heer has developed a very distinctive technique of camel hair tattooing. Even in his 50s, the artist is fully committed to pursue the adorable art and has complete mastery over the use of scissors in carving intricate hair motifs. He observes the body of camel as a canvas of unseen patterns which he intuitively follows while cutting its hair. He works without the aid of any preliminary sketch and uses his hands and fingers as the best tools to measure the spaces in between

[43]. Nazir Heer (camel hair tattoo artist) in discussion with the author, February 2014.

motifs and patterns (figure 23). He often uses sharp blades of his scissors to measure the distances between the motifs and patterns just by carefully touching the tips of its blades. Interestingly, when the process of intuitive cutting goes on, the herbivore feels no fear of the sharp blades and remains seated calmly in the same posture for hours.

Figure 23. Floral Motif encircled by the Triangular Band

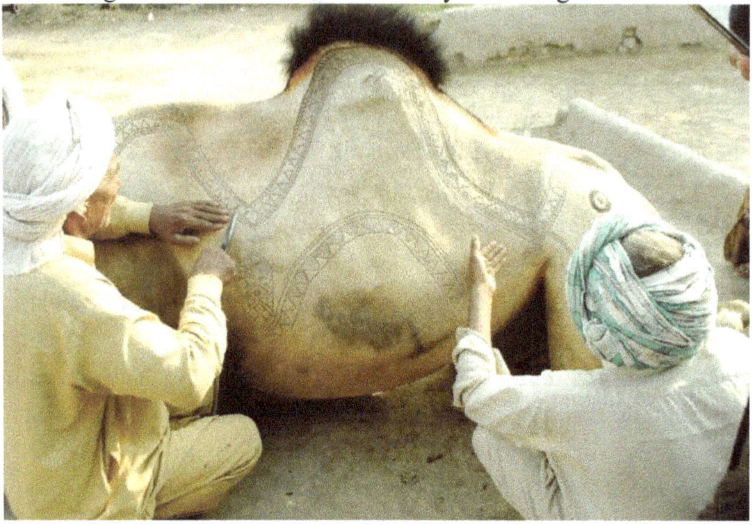

Source: Photograph by Muhammad Shafeeq, Ahmad Pur, Cholistan 2014.

Heer on the right using his left hand fingers to measure distance between the two triangular bands. Muhammad Ramzan on the left is acting as his apprentice.

Like other artists of camel hair tattoo, Nazir Heer has used no conventional ruler during the hair tattoo practice throughout his life. He begins the process of hair tattooing by cutting the hair on the camel's torso into curved and wavy lines following its body contours. Heer tactfully cuts the parallel lines which are later surmounted by small triangles. The dimensions of the triangles are kept equal by using the scissors' blades as measuring tools. He gently presses his left index finger on the scissors blades in the direction of each triangular pattern to maintain the flow of hair cutting (figure 24). Heer intuitively cuts with complete control over the scissors making patterns and motifs on various planes of the muscular and bony parts of the camel. By applying less pressure on the scissors a little darker tone of the hair is achieved. Whereas, to achieve the natural tone of darkest color the hair need to be cut closer to the skin to show up the darker tone of the bare body. This darker tone works as a negative space to accent the motifs.

Figure 24. Floral Motif encircled by the Triangular Band

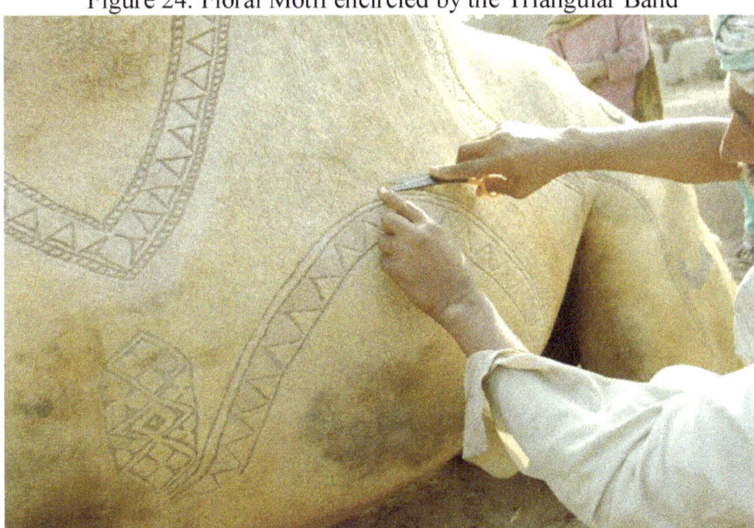

Source: Photograph by Muhammad Shafeeq, Ahmad Pur, Cholistan 2014.

Heer pressing his left index finger to facilitate hair cutting.

The camel coat after the initial trimming done by the barber, leaves the hair in various lengths at different places. The length ranges from one fourth of an inch (two points) to an inch depending on the body planes and contours. Next, it is the job of the tattoo artist to create motifs on the trimmed hair coat of the camel. Nazir Heer cuts the camel's hair in three different lengths which we can call levels. For level one cutting he cuts about ¼ of hair length and leaves ¾ there with the skin, for level 2 he cuts about half of hair length and leaves half there, and for level 3 he cuts about ¾ of the hair length and leaves ¼ there with the skin (figure 25).

Figure 25. Heer Trimming the Hair

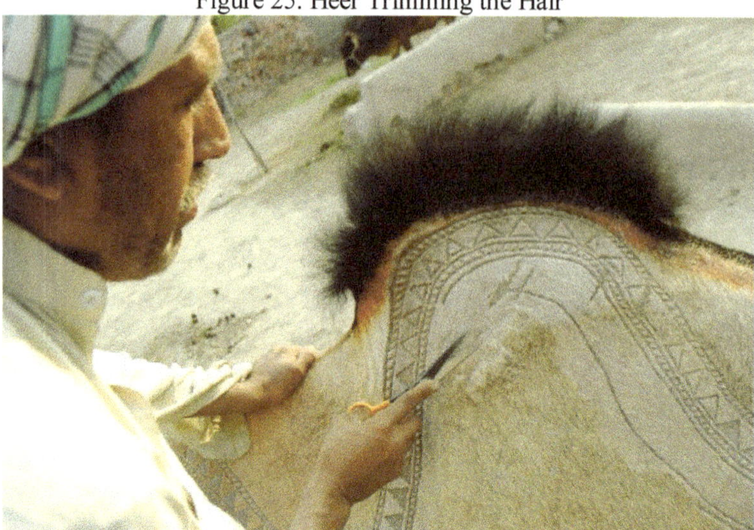

Source: Photograph by Muhammad Shafeeq, Ahmad Pur, Cholistan. 2014
Heer trimming the hair coat to prepare even base for hair tattooing.

To make it easy for the reader to understand as to how Nazir Heer cuts the camel coat in three levels creating different shades, we take the example where camel coat is about half inch (four points) thick. For level one cutting, he cuts away just one point (1/8th of an inch) of hair length and leaves three points (3/8th of an inch) of hair with the skin. At level two, Nazir cuts two points (1/4th of an inch) of hair length and leaves two points (1/4th of an inch) of hair length with the skin. For level three he cuts as close to the skin as possible and cuts away the 3 points (3/8th of an inch) of hair length leaves only hair length of one point (1/8th of an inch) with the skin. This level three cutting is considerably easier due to its closeness with the skin and is often delegated to the apprentice. The ratio of cutting hair coat for the three levels remains the same throughout the whole body of camel for the varying thickness of the hair coat. Although these three levels of cutting camel coat add complexity to the job of camel hair tattoo art but they give more beauty to the motifs.

Nazir Heer (or more appropriately his apprentice) cuts the outer edges for the motifs cutting the hair as close to the skin as possible which makes them appear dark and prominent; that is level three cutting. The inner parts of the motifs are trimmed in the middle tone and that is level two cutting. Level one cutting is used to make the coat even and the hair of irregular lengths are cut down which in fact were left by the barber in the initial trimming. Level one cutting is required mostly at the hump where hair are generally longer.

This style of cutting hair at three levels that Nazir Heer follows demands more time and effort and is usually beyond the approach of most of the artists. The tribes dwelling deep into the heart of Cholistan usually just cut the lines along the skin without any intricate details using just level three cutting.

The level three cutting creates the effect of negative areas which accent the positive parts of the motifs and divides the hair coat in to light and dark tones. The hard and coarse lines achieved in hair cutting resemble the hard lines of a carved wooden sculpture and for that reason the art can also be claimed as the art of camel carving. Nazir Heer opined that the artists who reside near Marut use the oldest patterns of hair tattoo art particularly those of Allah Dhawaya Paryar of Chak 40 Marut. He claimed that motifs of the artists there are quite bold and sharp.[44] Allah Dhawaya Paryar did not practice hair tattoo in that season as the camels of his patrons had caught cold in the tough winter season.

Heer has a unique choice of composing hair cut motifs and patterns. Inspired from the Pakistani flag, he likes to cut five pointed star and the crescent as a mark of patriotism. He cuts the animated motifs such as birds and animals on the lower body parts of the camel and he also cuts them in a relatively smaller size. He particularly also likes to cut the living imagery in an abstract manner to emphasize only the basic geometry of the birds and animals. He believed that as a Muslim he is not allowed to use animated imagery but he also admitted that if the patron demanded from him to cut any bird or animal he complied though with a tinge of guilt. In such a situation he draws the sketch of the animated imagery with the help of a marker on the camel's body. The commonly demanded animated motifs include the images of camels, lions, tigers, parrots, doves, sparrows, peacocks, and eagles.

Nazir Heer finds the shoulder blade of the camel most interesting part of the body. That is the reason he gets stimulated to cut distinct floral motifs on the higher parts of the shoulder blade (figure 26). Heer cuts floral motifs having six petals on either side of both the shoulders keeping little variation in the shape of petals to show movement. He also focuses to cut in hair coat the triangular bands mounted with sequence of small squares encircling the curve of the camel's belly. He further divides the layers of motifs into the forms of heart shape, squares, stars, triangles and floral motifs to enhance the effect of beauty (figure 27). These patterns are often used in a traditional manner by many other masters of camel hair tattoo art in Cholistan. He argued that the geometrical and organic designs of the traditional cloths of Cholistan are also a source of inspiration for his linear explorations in hair tattooing. He also gets influences from the patterns painted in

[44]. Nazir Heer (camel hair tattoo artist) in discussion with the author, February 2014.

bright colors on camel carts. The camel carts, Heer disclosed, are prepared in a village named 13 Sulang near Chak 11 Bahawalpur City, which is a popular center for production and decoration of animal carts.[45] Various motifs of camel hair tattoo art resemble the intricate floral designs which are painted on these carts (figure 28). These designs on wooden carts are also cut into various thin metal and bright colored plastic sheets (figure 29). Interestingly, the similar curved lines of camel hair tattoo art were also observed on the mud walls of the home of Muhammad Ramzan who has been discussed earlier (figure 30).

Figure 26. Floral Pattern

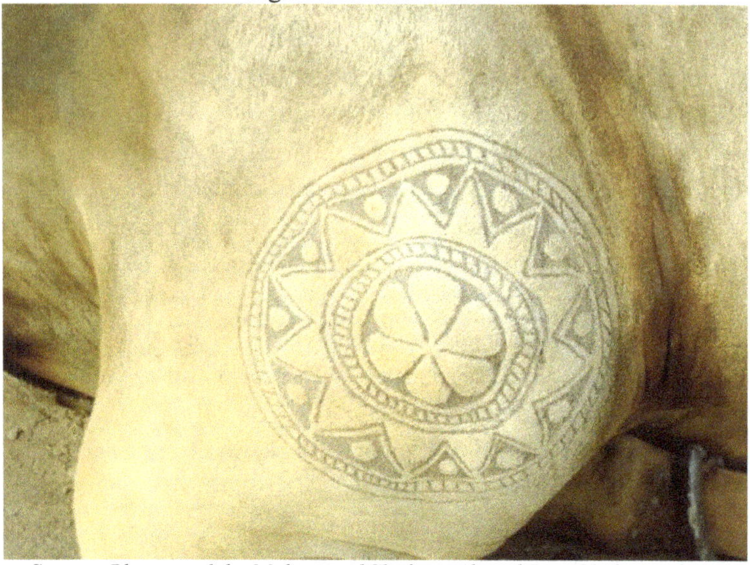

Source: Photograph by Muhammad Shafeeq, Ahmad Pur, Cholistan. 2014
Triangular Bands surmounting the Floral Motif

[45]. Nazir Heer (camel hair tattoo artist) in discussion with the author, February 2014.

Figure 27. Various Patterns of Camel Hair Tattooing

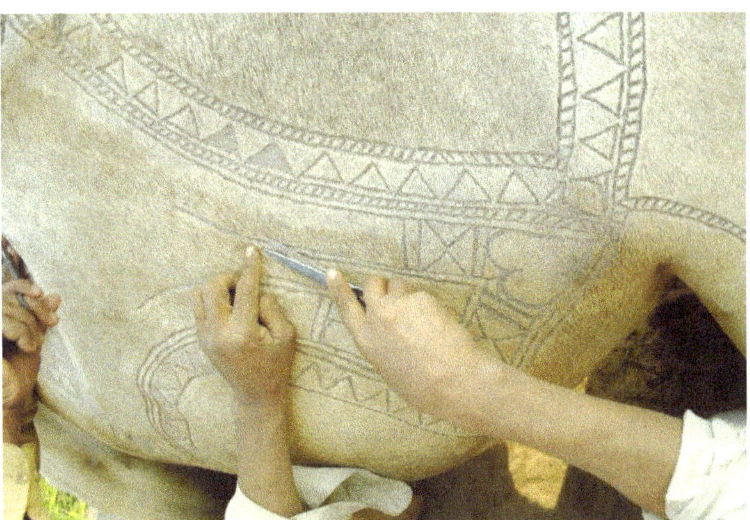

Source: Photograph by Muhammad Shafeeq, Ahmad Pur, Cholistan 2014. Heart- shaped motif, square bands and triangular motifs.

Figure 28. Painted Part of the Camel Carts

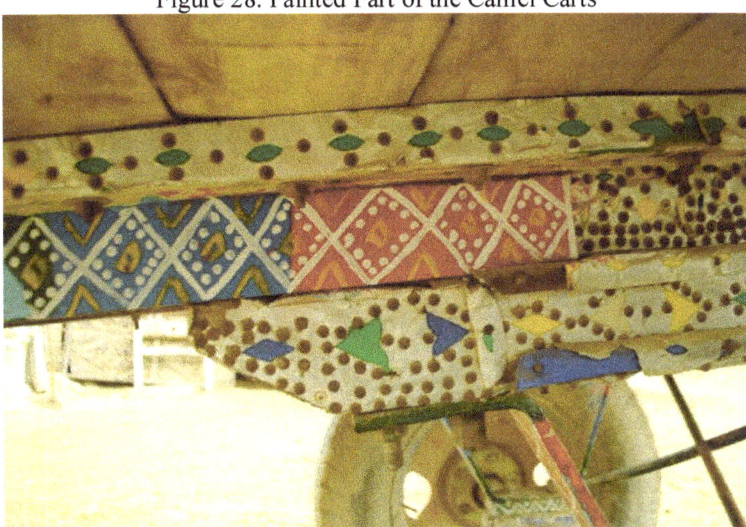

Source: Photograph by Muhammad Shafeeq, Bahawalpur City, Cholistan 2013. Similar heart- shaped motifs, square bands, and triangular patterns on the lower part of the cart.

Figure 29. Various Patterns of Camel Hair Tattooing

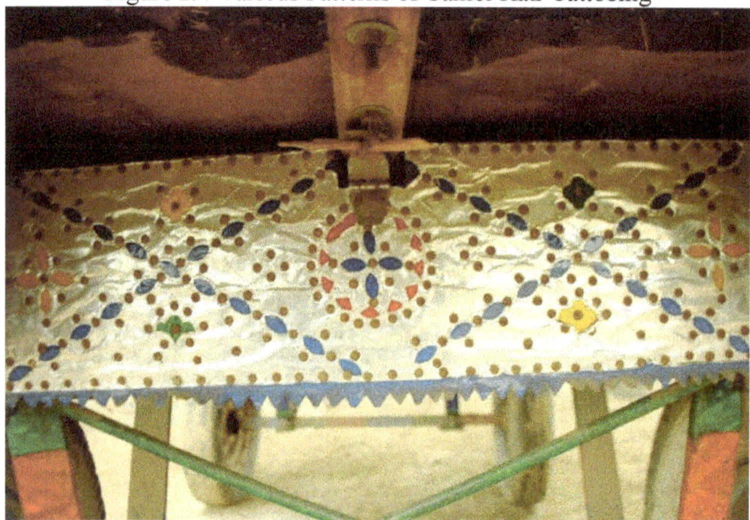

Source: Photograph by Muhammad Shafeeq, Bahawalpur City, Cholistan 2013. Floral motifs, squares divisions resemble camel hair tattoo motifs.

Figure 30. Curved Lines on the Walls of a Mud House

Source: Photograph by Muhammad Shafeeq, Bahawalpur City, Cholistan 2013. Cured lines of the mud houses resemble the parabola shape of camel hair tattoo.

Heer claimed that he had a great influence of the vegetation he observed around the desert. He is inspired by the flowers and leaves of various shapes and textures. Significantly, the heart shape leaf of the betel (*paan*) plant is one of his favorite motifs. He likes to compose the beautifully cut shape of the heart at the corner of the bulging belly to highlight the deep cuts of the camel. Heer composed one side of the camel in linear and geometrical patterns and the other side in curved and floral designs with little repetition to visually balance both the sides of the camel. He emphasized that the triangular patterns have been an essential part of all his compositions. Also he accentuated the significance of having a peaceful mind to create a beautiful hair tattooed camel and rubbished away the suggestion of using modern equipment like electric trimming machines for its practice.

Heer began his camel hair cutting by marking the hump of the camel with three dots each on either side of the camel's body as a reference for all the later developments. Right side of the camel is taken first to begin with. A dot is marked at the highest point of the hump and the second and third dots are marked lower part of the hump just where the hump begins to take form. These dots are marked in a way that they form the vertices of an imaginary triangle. Similarly, three dots are marked on the left side of the camel's torso.

Nazir Heer cuts the small triangular forms on the prominent curves of the body of the camel including the hump, hind quarters and shoulder blades on both sides. The triangles are about one inch wide and the height is also about one inch. These triangles are cut according to the body curves of the camel but ideally Nazir Heer tries to cut equilateral triangles. He cuts another band shaped like a horseshoe (parabola) which is filled with triangles (figure 31). At a gap of half an inch on the outer edge of this band runs another parallel band of similar thickness filled with heart shapes, floral forms, triangles and squares.

Figure 31. Horseshoe or Parabola Shape

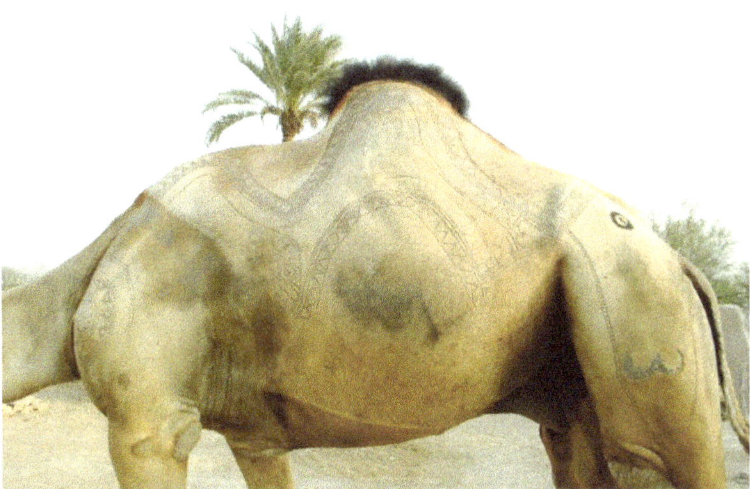

Source: Photograph by Muhammad Shafeeq, Ahmad Pur, Cholistan 2014.

Nazir Heer uses 10 to 15 sharpened iron scissors for cutting hair of one adult camel. A pair of sharp scissors hardly lasts a few hours and gets blunted. Then, at the end of the day the scissors again have to be sent to the village smith nearby for sharpening. These scissors have long and sharpened blades appropriate for cutting the intricate motifs and patterns. All the pairs of scissors that Nazir Heer used were observed to be almost of the same size and quality. Interestingly, Nazir Heer during the interview mentioned an ill-tempered camel that did not allow anyone to cut his hair. That poor soul had to be tied up with a cart and Heer had to patiently sit on that cart and cut the hair patterns with great difficulty.[46]

Heer argued that the skin color of the camel changes when the gigantic animal exerts physically. This results in dark and accented tones of the hair cut motifs and patterns. This could perhaps be due to increased flow of blood showing dark appearance of the skin exposed by hair cutting. Heer claimed that he uses the natural dye of red *henna* to accent the hair cut patterns and the surrounded areas of bare skin. He uses red *henna* at the ridge of the hump and just underneath that he uses black hair dye to enhance the beauty of camel hair tattoo motifs. Also, the bulging eyes of the camel look beautiful with the application of red *henna* and black hair dyes (figure 32).[47]

Figure 32. Applications of Henna Dye to Beautify Camel

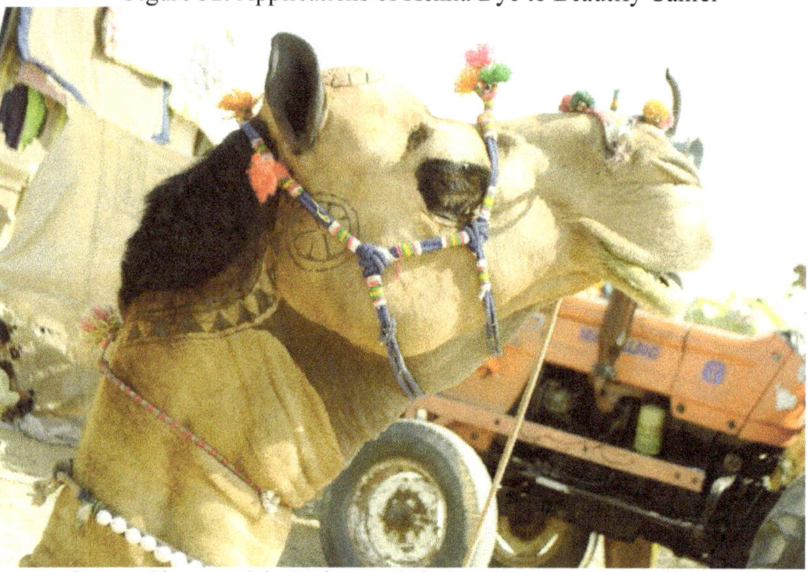

Source: Photograph by Muhammad Shafeeq, Channan Pir, Cholistan 2014.

[46]. Nazir Heer (camel hair tattoo artist) in discussion with the author, February 2014.

[47]. Nazir Heer (camel hair tattoo artist) in discussion with the author, February 2014.

During the interviewing, Nazir Heer explained that the camel owner Muhammad Ramzan had requested him to cut the patterns of two loving birds. Heer informed that he would cut them facing each other on a tree with branches spreading out to depict the supremacy of love in nature. His plan was to depict the pair of birds on the hind quarter to represent the inner shy and devoted feelings of the Ruhilas. It is pertinent to mention here that all camels in Cholistan bear a permanent totem mark on one of their hind quarters. Nazir Heer explained that he would compose this incised mark with the bird motifs to create another dimension.[48] He also feels inspired from the hardy plant of *Aak* (Calotropis Procera) widely present in the desert of Cholistan. It has purple and white colored flowers having five pointed petals resembling the shape of a star.

The artists of camel hair tattoo art frequently use five pointed stars on the hump of the camel to signify its universal supremacy over the other motifs and symbols (figure 33). Despite his illiteracy, Nazir Heer has the insight of a philosopher. He claimed that the camel is like a sky for him and the Creator has guided him to use the motifs of stars and the Moon which follows the setting of the universe. Therefore, he places the motifs of stars and the Moon up on the hump of the camel to depict their allegorical and spiritual significance. He portrays the star symbols varying in the number of points from 4 to 12, where its variation is fulfilling the demands of the overall compositions of the camel hair tattoo art. The camel hair art patrons also play a minor role in selecting some of the symbols and motifs with their suitable positions following the body of the camel.

Figure 33. Henna Dye applied to Accent Cosmic Symbols on the Hump

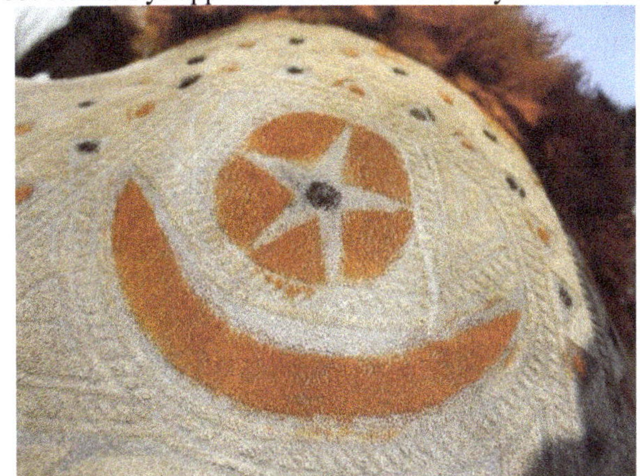

Source: Photograph by Muhammad Shafeeq, Channan Pir, Cholistan 2014.

[48]. Nazir Heer (camel hair tattoo artist) in discussion with the author, February 2014. For

Nazir Heer believed that for the past centuries, the Ruhilas have been observing the cosmic constellations of the Sun, the Moon and the stars. They used to keep a track of the stars in the sky as they travelled at night to avoid the scorching sun in the day. Also, the North Star was observed to find the right direction for their journey at night. The Ruhilas used to keep record of time by calculating the number of the appearances of full moon. They also believed on observing fate, a good or bad omen, marriage celebrations and seasonal festivals with the help of shining stars.

Heer claimed that very few Ruhilas with dedication and talent have the courage to learn the difficult and complicated art of camel hair tattoo. Of his dozen or so students only two or three have learned the hair tattoo art of camels with true conviction. While answering about the availability of camels, he informed that major areas of camel concentration in Cholistan are Mithra, Yazman, Latan, Khutri Bangla, Miranian and Marut. He disclosed that people enthusiastically participate in the *urs* of Hazrat Qaim Hussain Malang Nurani Shirazi near Yazman, which is also called Maila Latan Haar Shinghaar, held in the beginning of November every year. Nazir Heer added that the areas adjoining Derawar Fort are the oldest centers of camel hair tattoo activities in Cholistan where camels are also trained for various activities like camel riding, racing, and dancing. Khutri Bangla, Miranian and Marut are also popular camel hair tattooing spots. He further added that the Char Chak festival near Marut falling next to Kalay Par village area begins after the celebration of Channan Pir's 5th Thursday. Heer informed that Allah Wasaya Bohar, a famous hair tattoo artist will be there at Channan Pir to show his camel riding and tattooing talents. He further added that the artists belonging to the *Bhand* caste in Marut cut very different motifs using bold forms which seem to be inspired from the jewelry designs of Cholistan.[49]

While cutting the camel's hair coat, Nazir Heer seemed to be guided by his subconscious self with his mind in total control. With the pair of scissors his hand moved up and down as if floating over the ripples of water in a calm lake. It seemed as if he was in a trance and my occasional questions did not have any effect on his work. This is something that can only be achieved through years and years of dedication and devotion. His continuing discussion took him to the popular Punjabi folk love-story of Heer-Ranjha, in which Heer, sacrificed her life for her beloved Ranjha. Nazir Heer, whose last name incidentally is namesake of the female protagonist in the folklore, appreciated the devotion of Heer for her

---

[49]. Nazir Heer (camel hair tattoo artist) in discussion with the author, February 2014.

lover Ranjha. For Nazir Heer, Heer in the folklore stands as a symbol of love for the Divine.

For the symbols and motifs Nazir Heer claimed to draw inspiration from the numerals, letters and symbols drawn by the Sufis on the *taweez.* In the local Islamic tradition, a *taweez* is a piece of cloth or paper inscribed with sacred holy verses, symbols and numerals. It is folded and kept in small case for wearing like a necklace as a blessing and good omen.[50] Similarly, the whole ornamentation of tattooed camels including the hair cutting artistry, silver or brass jewelry, and floral embroidery on the cloth of a camel symbolizes the true feelings of a disciple who spends all his resources to achieve happiness of his Sufi saint. Synonymously, Heer believed that the Sufi helps you find a channel to achieve the Divine proximity for eternal happiness.

Nazir Heer has a rare combination of exceptional artistry, incisive intellect, philosophical sensitivity and spiritual insight but still he has to live a life of modest means. His poverty does not allow him to get his children educated from private schools and they have to go to some ordinary government school which is one of the greatest regrets of his life. Unluckily, his wife has not permitted the children to learn the fascinating art of camel hair tattoo from their father. She believes that the art has a detrimental effect on the eyesight.[51]

VILLAGES AROUND DERAWAR FORT

Derawar Fort is undoubtedly one of the most popular centers of art activities in Cholistan. Around 300 Hijra (912–913 A.D.) it was built by Deva Rawal, a Bhatti Rajput who was the ruler of Cholistan, Bikaner and Jaisalmer to the towns of Multan and Bahawalpur. Later, Nawab Mubarak Khan Abbasi attacked the Rajputs and the present fort came under the possession of Muslim leadership in 1804. It pushed the Hindu leadership permanently from Derawar side which was at that time a very important caravan route along the Hakra bed of Cholistan.[52] The Derawar fort has lost much of its charm but still a few frescos, although deteriorated, are a reminiscence of its beautiful artistry.

On way to Derawar, Malik Allah Wasaya, a well-known artist of camel hair tattoo was interviewed at his residence at Bohar Ali village. He claimed himself to be highly skilled in the art of camel hair tattooing and training camels for dancing, riding and racing. Also present there was another artist of the art of

---

[50]. Nazir Heer (camel hair tattoo artist) in discu+ssion with the author, February 2014.

[51]. Nazir Heer (camel hair tattoo artist) in discussion with the author, February 2014.

[52]. Nurul Zaman Ahmad Auj, *Harappan Heritage* (Multan: Caravan Book Centre, 1998), 106.

camel hair tattoo and camel training named Wali Muhammad Bohar. At Bohar Ali, Malik Allah Wasaya showed the dance performances of his two camels decorated with jewelry and embroidered cloth with intricate motifs of circles, triangles and squares resembling the traditional camel hair art motifs. He claimed that Mianwali is a popular hub for making silver jewelry for the ornamentation of camels. The artist claimed that the camels enjoy dancing because of the melodious sounds of the bells of their foot dresses.[53]

THE ARTIST IQBAL DHAYA OF DERAWAR FORT VILLAGE

A few kilometers from the Derawar Fort is a village named Chak 126 Daira Nawab Branch where an artist named Iqbal Dhaya, aged about 45, resides and practices the camel hair tattoo art. He claimed to have stepped in to this fascinating art at the age of 12 and achieved complete mastery over the art in five years. Iqbal uses about 4 to 5 scissors which are all of equal sizes and are similar to the scissors used by others. He works without any assistant and takes about 10 days to finish the tattoo. The designs in his tattoos have thick and bold lines stressing the intricate geometry of the floral motifs. All his floral patterns are bold as compared to the motifs of Nazir Heer but still they amazingly follow the anatomy of the animal.

Although Iqbal Dhaya had learnt the art but has started to practice it professionally only about five years back. His teacher named Kiniyani belonged to Mianwali. He has developed into a well-known artist of his area and locals like to hire him for annual camel hair tattoo artistry of their camels. He strictly cuts only non-animated motifs following the Islamic teachings where it is forbidden to depict animated imagery. Particularly, he claims to use the beautiful patterns of chain-like turning lines, creepers (*wal da buta)*, date-palm leaves, and zigzag lines (*gudra* in the camel hair tattoo jargon). At the end he likes to cut the star symbols on the hump. He claimed that his motifs are inspired from the organic forms present in desert. All his intentions behind his camel hair tattoo endeavors are to prepare the camels with utmost beauty for paying homage to their beloved Sufi Channan Pir. He believes that the camels also pay homage (*salam*) to the Sufi saints to be blessed with health and longevity. He carefully chooses the best camels for the holy visit to the Sufi shrine. These camels are covered with intricate geometrical and floral motifs. He discussed that the other domestic camels are kept home and their hair are cut in relatively bold and simple lines.

---

[53]. Malik Allah Wasaya (camel hair tattoo artist) in discussion with the author, November 2013.

The lines are mostly diagonal and straight without any floral patterns. It showed that Iqbal Dhaya specified the floral motifs to depict the hidden and intense feelings of meditation and devotion.[54] For him the art of camel hair tattoo is not done merely for the worldly pleasures rather an inner drive to achieve the union with the Divine through the Sufi sage.

Muhammad Riaz, the patron of Iqbal Dhaya in camel hair tattooing, is also the resident of the same village a few kilometers from the Derawar Fort. Muhammad Riaz claimed himself to be the pioneer of patronizing camel hair tattoo art in his village. He argues that he is financing the art of camel hair tattooing for the past twelve years. On further enquiry he told that he had no interest in the rulers of Cholistan including the distinguished Abbasis Nawabs. He strongly focuses the happiness of his Sufi Channan Pir for whom he offers the sacrifice of a goat every year and distributes the meat among the poor at the shrine of the Sufi.[55] Muhammad Riaz always hires Iqbal Dhaya for camel hair tattooing without imposing any pressure of his personal choices. Iqbal Dhaya confirmed that they both are close friends and have similar interests.

Here, the vocabulary by Iqbal Dhaya is mentioned which is often used by the Ruhila artists while practicing the art of camel hair tattoo. Iqbal uses the Saraiki word "Gudra" most commonly while working because he often uses it to make the bones look more prominent and also repeat them encircling around the belly of the camel to give it a prominent look. The artist Iqbal Dhaya explained further that the artistic and scientific terminology amongst the locals of Cholistan is developed over the centuries in the local language of Saraiki. All the geometric and organic motifs mentioned by Iqbal Dhaya are often used by nearly all the Ruhila artists of camel hair tattoo art. In fact, the motifs are directly influenced from the nature around including the herbs and shrubs of Cholistan. Iqbal Dhaya mentioned some of the terms commonly used in the hair tattoo motifs include:

Gudra: patterns meaning zigzag patterns
Tori: sponge gourd
Khajur: a date plant tree
Paan: betel, meaning a plant with heart shaped leaves that are chewed in India and Pakistan
Saru: cypress

---

[54]. Iqbal Dhaya (camel hair tattoo artist) in discussion with the author, November 2013.

[55]. Muhammad Riaz (camel hair tattoo artist) in discussion with the author, November 2013.

Aak: calotropis procera, a wild plant having flowers with five petals resembling five pointed star symbols used in camel hair tattoos.[56]

Apart from Iqbal Dhaya and Muhammad Riaz there was another artist named Abdul Karim at his resident in a village opposite to Derawar Fort. He was well aware of the glorious past of the Abbasis Nawabs and disclosed that his master named Ahmad Bakhsh (late) was a renowned artist of camel hair tattoo art who served the Abbasis. He claimed that for the past seven generations his ancestors had been practicing the art of camel hair tattooing patronized by the Abbasis. The land on which his family still resides is the land of Abbasi lords. He claimed that Abbasis used to travel on the tattooed camels which were adorned by his ancestors. He added that the art of camel hair tattoo was in practice much before the arrival of the Abbasis to the Derawar region.[57]

Few of the natives surrounding the fort belong to Hindu ancestry but as they have intermingled with Muslims over the centuries they do not call themselves Hindus rather they claim to be from Sufi religion. One well-known figure of the community named Baggu Ram with his nephew Theeway Ram were interviewed in Baggu Ram's mud brick home opposite the Derawar Fort. He claimed that his community does not worship any statue of Hindu gods and goddesses but rather finds that objectionable. He revealed that they do respect the Hindu deities Ram and Sita. Furthermore, he disclosed that they follow the teachings of the great Muslim Sufis like Shaikh Abd ul-Qadir Jilani r.a. and some other Muslim saints living in Cholistan.[58] They celebrate their religious and cultural activities in a hall having an enclosed octagonal construction decorated with some photographs of Muslim and Hindu nobles. Their females wear traditional dresses of long skirts and small blouses resembling a typical Cholistani female but with an addition of a prominent round and flat nose-pin. At the time of meeting with Baggu Ram all the females of his family were wearing very bright red colored makeup including lipsticks and nail polishes. They were getting ready for a marriage ceremony which strongly reflected the pattern of Hindu culture in neighboring India. It concludes to the fact that apart from strong Islamic influences the Hindu cultural impact is also quite evident on the camel hair tattoo art.

---

[56]. Iqbal Dhaya (camel hair tattoo artist) in discussion with the author, November 2013.

[57]. Abdul Karim (camel hair tattoo artist) in discussion with the author, November 2013.

[58]. Baggu Ram and Theeway Ram (followers of Sufi religion) in discussion with the author, November 2013.

THE ARTIST GUL MUHAMMAD OF MOJ GARH FORT VILLAGE

On the way to the gorgeous Fort of Moj Garh about 98 kms away from Bahawalpur there is a tomb of Maruf Khan, the builder of the Moj Garh Fort and the famous ancestor of Abbasis family. There is a village at some distance from the fort which is abode to some of the best known artists of camel hair tattoo art. Most of the Ruhilas there have been trained by their elders in the art of camel hair tattoo since their childhood. Every year, they begin collectively the practice from the mid of March to celebrate the arrival of spring season. The most experienced and renowned artist amongst them is Gul Muhammad who is probably about a hundred years old and is considered the oldest surviving artist in the whole area. Gul Muhammad claimed that he belonged to Maral cast and his ancestors brought him in Cholistan after the first war of 1965 between India and Pakistan. The artist Gul Muhammad was introduced by Nabi Bakhsh, a native of Pamwar cast who has a shop of eatables next to the Moj Garh Fort.

During interview with Gul Muhammad he disclosed that for the past seven generations his forefathers have been practicing the art of camel hair tattoo. He is a well-versed with the art of camel hair tattoo and has original ideas about the techniques of his ancestral masters in the art. Here, some of his ancestral style and technical instructions are mentioned in order to understand his hair tattoo art in his own words.

"To begin hair tattooing, the artist combs the hair of the camel to keep the hair in one direction making an even base for hair cutting. Then, two scissors at the beginning are used to cut the hair in a particularly required direction. The basic sketch is never done on the body of the camel. The preliminary motifs of camel hair tattoo are always present in the mind of the artist without any need for specific and conscious preliminary drawings."

"The sets of scissors used are of the same size with considerably longer blades. These longer blades help cut in intricate designs which are not possible to cut with scissors having smaller blades. The rough and coarse hair of the camel do not allow smooth flow of cutting lines until and unless sharp scissors are used. To create a smooth effect of hair cutting a certain distance between the scissors and camel's body is maintained to achieve an even designed surface."

"The old technique of camel hair tattoo involved the use of brushes made of twigs of local trees. The artists of the yore used to chew twigs at one end of the branch to make brushes with natural flexible fibers for applying henna dye on camels after completing the hair cutting artistry. These brushes looked much similar to the modern soft painting brushes. The henna paste was prepared by mixing it in water to apply on the camel's body. Later, the dried thick dyes were washed with water leaving beautiful floral and geometrical motifs all around the body of the camels."

"Nowadays, camel hair tattoo artists do not go for complex techniques of preparing brushes from trees and instead buy the readily available commercial painting brushes. In fact, most of the artists use the chemically prepared hair dye named Kala Kola to apply on the hair of the camel for the reason that it lasts a good six months and that is considerably longer than the natural henna dye that lasts for about three months."[59]

Even in this day and age, the whole family of Gul Muhammad resides in a structure made up of straw, branches of trees, dried shrubs and some strips of cloth knotting them up to sustain the structure. What is even more amazing is that they all seem to live very contented and happy lives. At a philosophical level, their lives are an ample proof that happiness is not dependent upon materials that we the ordinary mortals spend all our lives to attain.

Camel milk is an important part of their daily diet. The wife of Gul Muhammad, who claimed to be about forty years younger than him told that her sons Khan Muhammad, Jan Muhammad and Nur Muhammad were trained by their father in the art of camel hair tattoo following their centuries old ancestral heritage. She informed that her sons will start camel hair tattoo art on the first day of the appearance of full moon of the spring season which falls in the early days of March to celebrate the arrival of spring season. She claimed that her sons use floral and geometrical motifs in camel hair tattoo art to symbolize devotion and respect for their Sufi Channan Pir.

They visit Channan Pir every year with their beautifully adorned hair tattooed camels and a goat. The goat is slaughtered and sacrificed there and its meat cooked in the utensils provided by the organizers of the Sufi shrine and it is distributed amongst the poor. One could only wonder in amazement at the very thought that there could be people poorer than the Gul Muhammads. And, also that if there could be anybody in this world more generous than these folks. That is perhaps their humble way of being thankful to Allah for whatever that they have been bestowed with. I thought for a while that the spiritually impoverished people living and enjoying the comforts of life in metropolitan cities would perhaps be able to match these simple people in aspects of magnanimity and generosity.

---

[59]. Gul Muhammad (camel hair tattoo artist) in discussion with the author, November 2013.

She also pointed out some other popular camel hair tattoo artists named Allah Ditta and Fatih Muhammad who live in their neighbors and claimed that all men here in their village have complete mastery over camel hair tattoo art.[60]

A few meters away from Gul Muhammad's residence some mud houses and cemented rooms belonged to the family of Illahi Bakhsh. Illahi Baksh was about 40 years old and learned the art of camel hair tattoo from his grandfather Bakhsh Midan who was about 80 years old. Illahi Bakhsh claimed that the art of camel hair tattoo is older than Maruf Khan of Moj Garh Fort. Midan also believed that Moj Garh Fort for to be about 400 years old and the art of camel hair tattoo was in practice much before. He indicated that the art of camel hair tattoo might be about 6 to 700 years old.[61] Here, it is significant to mention that Abdul Kareem of Derawar Fort village also claimed that the art of camel hair tattoo is much older than the Abbasis in the Cholistan region. If these accounts are taken to be true then the art of camel hair tattoo was perhaps in practice at the time of Bhatti Rajas or even much before when caravans moved on route along the dried Hakra River.

Interestingly, Illahi Bakhsh added another fact that the linear pattern on the traditional *ralli* cloth has the patch work lines of embroidery which inspires the artist of camel hair tattoo art. The *ralli* cloth he mentioned looks much similar to camel hair tattoo art as it also involves the details of cutting and designing. Also, the square and triangular patches on the *ralli* with floral motifs closely resemble the symbols and motifs of camel hair tattoo art. In addition, Illahi Bakhsh claimed that camel artists charge about 4,000 in Pakistani rupees and take 5 to 6 days to complete the process of hair tattooing of a camel. He further added that the Sun, the Moon and the stars symbolize the Divine supremacy over creations which the camel hair tattoo artists portray in their art by not cutting these symbols on the lower parts of the camel's body. The reason he believed that these symbols if drawn on the lower body parts, would lose their supremacy when they would fall into contact with the sand and dirt which would not to be a good omen for both the artist and the patron. Therefore, the camel hair tattoo artists cut such sacred symbols of the Divine power on the top most part of the camel that is the hump which symbolizes the entire setting of the universe for them. They also like to create floral motifs which may take four to five days to complete but simpler lines may take only two days.

---

[60]. Gul Mohammad's wife (wife of a camel hair tattoo artist) in discussion with the author, November 2013.

[61]. Illahi Bukhsh & Bukhsh Midan (camel hair tattoo artists) in discussion with the author, November 2013.

THE ARTIST BAKHSH MIDAN

The grandfather of Illahi Bakhsh named Bakhsh Midan, one of the most experienced artist of the region revealed that he preferred the motifs of rooster, peacock and camel. That clearly was in stark contrast to the widely believed boundaries set in Islam that forbid using living imagery in art. He was also fond of making human portraits, significantly those of the patrons, on the front shoulder blade of the camel but preferably in an abstract manner and not in realistic style. Though not for the animal imagery, he exercised restraint in making human figures in line with his inner Islamic belief.[62] It seems pertinent to mention here that Hindu influences of creating animated imagery in art are observed much stronger at Moj Garh Fort. This could be explained to be the result of the proximity to the porous Pak-India border. These camel hair tattoo spots have Hindu settlements much similar to the ones near the Derawar Fort.

Additionally, the old fellow Bukhsh Midan claimed that they all visit the annual festival of Sufi Inayat Shah at his sacred shrine in Layyah to pay tribute to the revered Sufi. It takes them about 5 to 6 hours to reach Layyah by bus where the celebrations start every year from the 14th night of the lunar month of falling in the spring season. The festival lasts for about 8 days starting few days after the 5th Thursday of Channan Pir festival. Apart from spirituality, Midan claimed that the annual festival at Layyah is also arranged for selling and purchasing of camels. He informed that many foreigners visit the festival from Egypt, India and Middle East to buy the trained camels in the art of dancing and racing. There the hair tattooed art camels display talents and beauty to fascinate the visitors of the Sufi festivals.[63]

THE CHANNAN PIR FESTIVAL

The most popular figure of respect for the people of Cholistan is Sufi Channan Pir. The mystic saint belonged to a village located deep inside Cholistan region that is now named after the saint. This village is located between Derawar and Din Garh forts in the Cholistan desert about 60 kilometers from Bahawalpur. There is a large shrine of Channan Pir constructed with a mosque for the devoted disciples and visitors. Thousands of Ruhilas take their elegantly tattooed camels to visit the shrine every year (figure 34). On one hand they use the hair tattooed camels as an ostentatious model to joyfully celebrate the arrival of spring and on the other hand for pay homage to the native Sufi. The camels covered with intricate motifs

---

[62]. Bakhsh Midan (camel hair tattoo artist) in discussion with the author, November 2013.
[63]. Illahi Bakhsh (camel hair tattoo artist) in discussion with the author, November 2013.

and symbols look majestic while showing various skills in the grand festivals organized near the Sufi shrine. Surprisingly, no female could be seen in the camel activities of racing, riding and dancing. The male oriented society of Ruhilas does not allow any female to see the performances of their camels. The women and young children are invited to attend only the religious festivals arranged at the Sufi shrines. The Ruhilas visit from faraway places with all their family members to seek blessings and offer sacrifices of their domesticated goats.

Figure 34. Tattooed Camels at Channan Pir

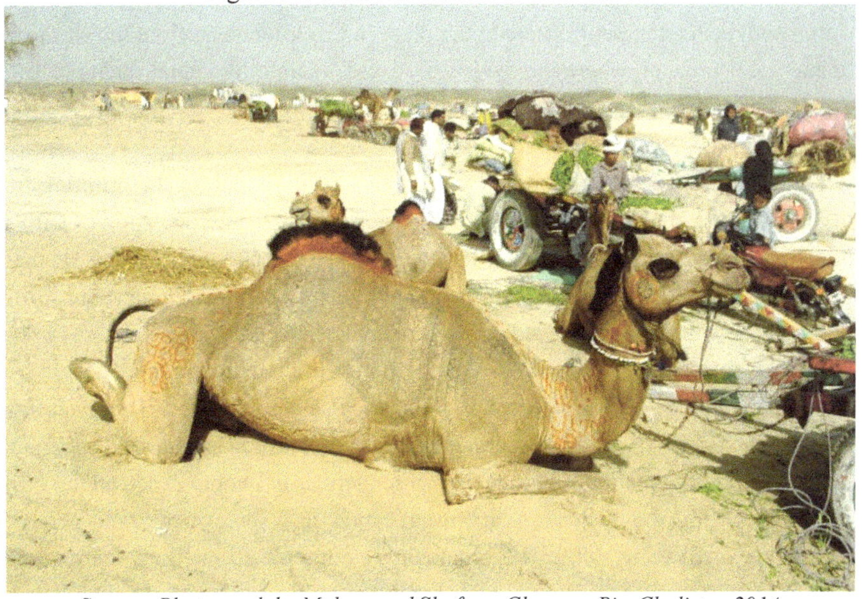

Source: Photograph by Muhammad Shafeeq, Channan Pir, Cholistan 2014.

The Sufi Channan Pir has been considered a spiritual model for the disciples to earnestly beseech forgiveness, health and wealth and also to be bestowed with baby boys. In the Ruhilla culture sons are considered to be much more worthy than daughters. As a mark of respect the hair tattooed camels are also adorned with silver jewelry to offer tribute to the great Sufi. The devotees arrive at the holy shrine of the Sufi sage in the form of processions capturing the whole splendor of the desert. The creatively tattooed hairy body of the camel gives effects of woven carpets interspersed with spiritual gestures. The devotees of Sufi Channan Pir use various means of transportation including camels, horses, ox-carts, trucks, vans, busses, motorbikes and even on foot to reach the holy shrine. On the eve of sixth and seventh Thursdays of the festival, the shrine of the sage is densely occupied with the devotees. Every year the enthusiastic Ruhilas bring along the sacrificial animals and also the cooking utensils for cooking and distributing food at the shrine. The shrine owners also keep the necessary utensils to give them to any one for cooking. Interestingly, these visitors seem very excited raising voices in hazy and dusty atmosphere of the desert to show their love and dedication. Some devotees walk bare foot to the sacred place on the hot and thorny desert dunes without any fear of hurting themselves. They all gather around the shrine in the form of a grand *maila* celebrated on seven consecutive Thursdays spanning from end of February to the beginning of April every year. The fifth Thursday is considered the most inviting because of the grand camel riding and racing competitions that take place, a few kilometers from the shrine at 'dahar' of Cholistan, where the land is hard and suitable for camel racing. These camel racing events are claimed to have been taking place for the past fifteen years.

The traditional celebration of camel racing continues from the morning till the late afternoon. The two competitive groups ride on camel carts along with a huge procession of folks travelling on bikes, rickshaws and carts raising slogans in favor of their respective teams. The race begins from a marked portion of the *dahar* to the straight opposite side. The race creates a hustling scene where all the participants of the race make their camels run at the maximum speed. The race track spans about ten kilometers and finishes in a few minutes. The awarding committee comprising of senior organizers observes the race standing on camel carts at the ending marks. As the race a large number of people dance on the beat of the *dhol* for the victorious duo, the camel and its owner, with a large procession of dancing folks. The organizing committee formally announces the winner interestingly there is no monetary reward for the winner, just a white cloth about 1.5 meters by 1 meters which is tied around the neck of the winning camel. The victorious rider on his magnificent camel proudly rides around the judges and other participants to show his superb mastery which brings great honor to his respective tribe.

The camel cart races take about one whole day and as the evening time approaches all the participants, organizers and visitors move to pay tribute to their honorable Sufi sage Channan Pir to seek Divine blessings. The camels specified for racing and dancing are nearly all covered with the motifs and symbols rooted in Islamic spiritualism. The hair tattoo artists express through their unique styles a diverse range of mystical symbols to symbolize the Divine supremacy by depicting the universal bodies including a moon, star and the Sun in their art. These cosmological symbols are generally composed on the hump of the camel following their highest placement in the order of the universe. These astronomical symbols of camel hair tattoo art signify the conscious mind of the tattoo artist who purposely uses these rhythmic symbols wrapped in the spiritual codes of Islam.

CHAPTER 4

The Spiritual Aspects of Camel Hair Tattoo Art

Camel hair tattoo art is practiced upon the arrival of the spring season. It's the time when the Ruhilas participate in the traditional festivals and congregate at the shrine of their beloved Sufis. The hair tattoo artists depict various vegetal and geometric motifs cut in hair and then paint with the natural dye of henna to accent the aesthetical and mystical qualities. The camel tattoo artist experiences a certain connection with God to explore His creations in the form of intricate lines and forms cut in the hard hair of the camel. The deep lineation in hair depicts his intense feelings not solely for the sake of artistic beauty but also for the attainment of his spiritual ecstasy. The humble hair tattoo artist of the desert does not portray himself physically anywhere in his tattoos; he instead focuses the supremacy of God through the universal symbols of the Sun, the Moon and the stars. He depicts a certain world of hair tattoo motifs and symbols onto the body of the gigantic camel to seek the happiness of his Sufi saint who stands as a symbol of Divine blessings for him. The Sufi saint though passed away centuries ago is alive for him.

A seventeenth century Turkish Sufi, Muhammad Al Jerrahi rightfully quoted Sarraj's classical definition of Sufism in the book titled, *Essential Sufism.* Sarraj claimed that Sufis are the people who prefer God to everything and God prefers them to everything else.[64] Also, the author mentioned the words of his Sufi teacher Muzaffer Ozak to highlight the significance of Islamic teachings in paving way for Sufism. "Sufism without Islam is like a candle burning in the open without a lantern. There are winds which may blow that candle out. But if you have a lantern with glass protecting the flame, the candle will continue to burn safely," he added.[65] Therefore, the essence of Sufism is present in the light of Islamic teachings within which the camel hair tattoo artist has grown up. Although, he does not have access to modern school education he attains his spiritual illumination from the Quranic teachings which are his sole source of

---

[64]. James Fadiman and Robert Frager ed., *Essential Sufism* (New Jersey: Castle Books, 1998), 2.

[65]. James Fadiman and Robert Frager ed., *Essential Sufism* (New Jersey: Castle Books, 1998), 4.

learning. He considers himself fortunate to have evaded the modern society of materialism and has rather learnt to enlighten himself with the spirit of Islam. This general isolation from the contemporary society makes him oblivious of the material objects and he develops a lack of desire for worldly things. These factors together develop a leaning towards spiritualism.

In her book *Islam and Art* the author, Lois Lamya al-Faruqi, has highlighted a particular aspect of the Holy Quran for establishing the spiritual aspects of Islamic art. She argued:

> It is to the Quran the Muslims owe their greatest debt for their art, as well as for every other aspect of their lives.... In this single piece of literature (Holy Quran) the so called 'First work of art in Islam,' the Muslim found all the artistic principles he was to demand of his art objects, regardless of medium. Abstract content, non-developmental form, and the arabesque—they were all present in the holy book of Islam.[66]

Ever since the birth of Islam, the belief in the descended scripture of the Holy Quran opened new dimensions for the Muslim artist and guided his spirit with the essence of *Tauhid.* The concept of *Tauhid* meaning belief in one God, laid the foundations of geometric and abstract motifs and symbols. In fact, the teachings of Islam did not encourage to depict the living imagery in art but instead focused on the exploration of the hidden norms behind the mere representations. The author Lois Lamya al-Faruqi has beautifully briefed the concept of Muslim art as:

> The Islamic message of *Tauhid* is permeated with both the content and form of Islamic art. First in content, it can be demonstrated that Islamic art is primarily an abstract art. Since Allah (S.W.T.) is so complete other than the natural world, no creature from nature could stand as a symbol for Him.... Muslim artist makes use of motifs from the animal world... in such a way that even they express... that Allah (S.W.T.) is indeed infinite, totally transcendent, and inexpressible in natural terms. They become fantastic creatures divorced from creation.[67]

The Muslim art is throughout mystified with the belief in Oneness of God but the Muslim artist has never been inclined to depict God in any recognizable

---

66. Dr. Lois Lamya Al Faruqi, Islam and Art (Islamabad: National Hijra Council, 1985), 30.
67. Ibid., 20.

animated form. The artist did however, portray the spirituality behind the creations as the reflection of His omnipresence.

A renowned French theologian, John Calvin (1509- 1564) believed in the similar notions that God revealed Himself in the Holy Scripture and in the visible world of nature. His ideas have been pronounced in the beginning of the Confession of Faith during the Synod of Dordrecht (it was an assembly of Dutch Protestants held at the Reformed Church, Dordrecht in 1618–1619 to settle a divisive controversy):

> We know [God] by two means. Firstly, through the Creation, preservation and government of the entire world: because to our eyes this is like a beautiful book in which are all creatures, great and small, as if they were letters, showing us the invisible aspects of God, namely His eternal strength and Godhead .... Secondly, He reveals Himself yet more clearly and perfectly through His holy and Divine word.[68]

Likewise, God has given shape and structure to all His creations to symbolize His power and government over the universe. As He only knows where, what and when something has been created, therefore, only He Himself can describe it with utmost truth and perfection. The Muslims also refer to the Quranic teachings for better understanding of the Creator and His creations.

The word 'camel' appears in the Holy Quran twenty one times wherein it has been mentioned with various characteristics including his gigantic and unique humped body structure, significant role for the survival of human life in the desert, its ability to survive without much intake of water, innocent and humble character dominant with yellow-brown tones which are in harmony with the desert. Notably, no animal has been depicted as a symbol of Divine blessings other than the camel. The Holy Quran says, "And nothing has prevented Us from sending signs except that the former peoples denied them. And We gave Thamud the she-camel as a visible sign, but they wronged her. And We send not the signs except as a warning."[69]

Likewise in the Quran, Prophet Salih (A.S.) the messenger of Allah warned the people of Thamud as:

---

[68] Ibid.

[69]. Surat Al-Isra, Al-Quran, verses 59, http://Qur'ān.Com/17/59 (accessed November 21, 2014).

> And O my people! This she-camel of Allah is a symbol to you: leave her to feed on Allah's (free) earth, and inflict no harm on her, or a swift penalty will seize you![70]

It is quite significant to mention here that the camel has been used as a symbol of peace and kindness for all the humanity in the Quranic verses. The people of Thamud demanded from Prophet Salih (pbuh) that they would believe in his God if a pregnant she-camel would come out of the mountain there. Their improbable demand was miraculously fulfilled by Allah and the pregnant she-camel appeared. Despite having seen the miracle of Allah, the people of Thamud were adamant and unyielding. They tortured the miraculous she-camel to death and that resulted in inviting the wrath of Allah that annihilated the entire nation of Thamud. There is no other animal that has been given so much significance in the Holy Quran.

Apart from the Holy Quran, the Sunnah of the Holy Prophet Muhammad (pbuh) is the other source for the Muslims to seek spiritual knowledge and wisdom. The Prophet Muhammad (pbuh) followed the devoted path of the Divine and highlighted the significance of camels in his sayings called *hadith.*

The last Prophet of Allah, Muhammad (pbuh) had a she-camel called *al-Adba* which is mentioned in a *hadith* documented in *Sunnan-i abi Daud* (a collection of *ahadith*):

> The she-camel of the Messenger of Allah called al-Adba had not been outstripped by another, but an Arab came on a young riding camel of his and outstripped it. That distressed the companions of the Messenger of Allah (pbuh), but he said: It is Allah's right that nothing should become exalted in the world but He lowers it.[71]

This hadith shows that Holy Prophet (pbuh) admired his she-camel and at the time of her defeat in the race did not feel any distress. Notably, it also proved that the camel race was in fashion at the time of Prophet Muhammad (pbuh) in the 7th century A.D. Camel racing as practiced in Cholistan may have been introduced by the Arabs in the deserts of the subcontinent after the Arab invasion of Sind in 712 A.D.

---

70. Surah Hud, Al-Quran, verse 64, http://Qur'ānindex.net/kelime.php?id=7984 (accessed November 21, 2014).

71. See Sunnan-i abi Daud: General Behavior (Kitab Al-Adab), trans., Volume 42, Hadith 4784 http://sunnah.com/abudawud/43/30 (accessed November 12, 2014).

At the time of the conquest of Makkah in 629 A.D. (8th A.H.) Prophet Muhammad (pbuh) rode on his she-camel, named *al Qaswa* with his head bowed down in humility and modesty. He did not prefer to ride on a horse which at that time was considered a symbol of pomposity and pride. Prophet Muhammad (pbuh) entered the courtyard of the Holy Kaaba and circumambulated the sacred Kaaba on a camel.[72] It provides the evidence that a camel in Islam stands as a symbol of self-effacement and humility.

The ancient Hindu scriptures Manu-smriti (11:201) and Manu Samhita described that camel riding is forbidden for a Hindu Brahman and having its milk and meat is also strictly prohibited.[73] It may be concluded that camel is a sacred symbol for the Muslims and perhaps the same cannot be said for the Hindus. Later, after the advent of Islam, the Holy Quran and the *ahadith* of the Prophet Muhammad highlighted camel as a symbol of blessings and mercy. The absence of camel depictions in Hindu religious art and its prohibition for the elite class of Brahmans shows that the art of camel hair tattoo might have been initiated or at least popularized by the Muslims in recognition of its sacrosanct legacy in Islam.

The most eminent Sufi poet of Cholistan, Khawaja Ghulam Farid, who was a master of seven languages: Arabic, Persian, Urdu, Sindhi, Punjabi, Balochi and Marwari, and is popularly called as the only *Haft Zaban* poet (meaning poet of seven languages) depicted in his poetry purity and love found in the desert life. Khawaja Ghulam Farid believed that the ideal place for meditation is the desert of Cholistan because of its endless beauty and calm. He focused in his poetry the mortality of man and this world where every creature truthfully reflected the pure and immortal nature of the Divine. The sandy and dusty dunes of the desert of Rohi for him truly symbolized the dream-like worldly life which has no eternal reality but serves as a bridge between one's soul and the Divine. His poetry narrates the Sufi experience of losing one's self for the ultimate spiritual union with the One and the Absolute. One of the most popular verses of Khawaja Ghulam Farid's Ṣufi poetry go in praise of God, the English translation of which is like:

---

[72]. See Prophetic Timeline: Life of Prophet Muhammad S.A.W.W. (Seerah Resource, The Conquest of Makkah/ Year 8 AH), https://prophetictimeline.wordpress.com/2011/03/26/the-conquest-of-makkah-year-8ah/ (accessed November 13, 2014).

[73]. Ali Unal, *The Prophet Promised* (New Jersey: Tughra Books, 2013).

You Are My Ardour
You are my ardour, my friend, faith, creed.
You are my body, you are my spirit, heart, soul….[74]

Here, Khawaja Ghulam Farid has merged the elements of nature in his Sufi poetry as the depictions of natural love and devotion for the Divine. He made a melodious and harmonious amalgamation in his mystic poetry to mesmerize the listeners and the viewers. The place where Khawaja Farid meditated is now called *Jhok* Farid meaning the city of Farid. An annual three day *urs* (festival celebrating the death anniversary of the Sufi) of Khawaja Farid is organized in *Jhok* Farid, in District Rahim Yar Khan, every year which is also called *Rohi Maila*. During the day events like Sufi *Majlis* (a spiritual gathering where Sufi poetry is recited with or without music), wrestling, kabaddi, horse and camel racing and dancing, bike rallies, and *jhumar* dance are held. *Jhumar* is a traditional dance of Cholistan in which men dance and move in a circle on the beat of drum and as more and more men join, the circle expands. During the night the musicians sing the poetry of Khawaja Farid which the people of the Rohi throng to listen to. The singing event is of special significance for the camel hair tattoo patrons and artists. The message of love and devotion transcends into their hearts and minds. This spirit and intellect reflects in the abstract motifs and symbols of camel hair tattoo art. In fact, the well composed rhythmic intervals of Sufi poetry and hair artistry of the Cholistan both commonly share an intuitive empowerment that opens the dilemma of spirituality and tranquility.

Khawaja Ghulam Farid stated the mystical and thorny path of love. The translation of his verses says:

Love is a joy for heart broken
Most dependable perfect guide;
All the secrets love reveals
Which otherwise are denied.
Without my beloved I am lost
Without him what can I attain?[75]

The feelings of pure affection and meditation for the Divine is depicted in the form of a spiritual union between the lovers. In fact, this union is achieved

---

[74]. See Sufi Poetry: *Meda Ishq Vi Toon* by Khawaja Ghulam Farid. https://Şūfipoetry.wordpress.com/2009/11/03/meda-ishq-vi-toon/ (accessed December 2014).

[75]. Nurul Zaman Auj, *Harapan Heritage* (Multan: Caravan Book Centre, 1998), 266-67.

through a transformation from a worldly body of materialism to the real essence of asceticism. The natives of Cholistan for the past generations have been thronging the shrines of the Sufi saints to seek that finer vision of the Divine beauty. This beauty is their real destination which they try to reflect in the form of their beautifully and mystically tattooed camels that they take along to visit the Sufi shrine to pay homage to the Sufi. Traditional camel riding, racing, and dancing activities arranged at the shrine of the Sufi saint. Thousands of Ruhilas flock to the deep desert shrine of the most popular Sufi Channan Pir to commemorate the sacrifices of their Sufi in the holy path. The noble and graceful camels with hair cut bodies participate there as an ideal model to seek blessings. Similarly, the patterns and symbols on the bodies of the hair tattooed camels signify the physical and spiritual dimensions to depict the inner and hidden feelings of the camel hair tattoo artists. They feel great honor and privilege to follow the artistic legacy of their forefathers to create a unique amalgam of objective and subjective symbols of camel hair tattooing.

The German linguist and semiotician, Winfried Noth (b. 1944) mentioned that the medieval scholars argued about symbols as the phenomena of the world and also as a symbol of Divine meanings.[76] Here, in the camel hair tattoo art, the artist strives to use geometrical symbols of five, six or more pointed stars to depict creations and the supremacy of the Creator without any intention to portray the image of God. John Calvin (1509–1565) in his *Institutes of the Christian Religion,* which remains one of the foremost theological works in Protestant history, writes:

> We think it is unlawful to give shape to God, because God himself has forbidden it, and because it cannot be done without, in some degree, tarnishing his glory. ... And the majesty of God, which is far beyond the reach of any eye, must not be dishonored by unbecoming representations.[77]

Likewise, in the art of camel hair tattoo, the artist of the art acknowledges his limited self and explores symbols of organic and geometric nature he observes in Cholistan. The camel hair tattoo artists have intentionally rejected the realistic portrayal of living beings to depict their universal soul within. The rhythmic movements of the hair cutting lines and motifs smoothly merge into one another

---

[76]. Winfried Noth, *Handbook of Semiotics*. Bloomington: Indiana University Press, 1995, 116.

[77]. John Calvin, *Institutes of the Christian Religion* (Geneva, 1545), vol. I, chap. XI, para. 12 (ed. J.-D. Benoit [Paris, 1957]), 135.

along the contours of the huge camel as if the water of streams and rivers flow into an unfathomable sea.

Federico Zuccari (c. 1542–1609) an Italian Mannerist painter and architect has described the act of God as:

> But in forming this internal Design man is very different from God: God has one single Design, most perfect in substance, containing all things, which is not different from Him, because all that which is in God is God; man, however, forms within himself various designs corresponding to the different things he conceives. Therefore, his design is an accident, and moreover it has a lower origin, namely in the senses. [78]

Zuccari meant to consider nature which has been created under the Intellectual principle and formulated through the advancement of human logic perfect in its creation. While the acts of humans may be imperfect as they originate from the limited intellect and much ignorant senses of the humans. Similarly, the hair tattoo artists acknowledge the perfection of God's creations and try to symbolically follow the nature free of any doubt about the errors of visible reality.

Amazingly, the artists of camel hair tattoo commonly believed that their hair artistry serves as a kind of meditation for them without any ostentatious desires of this world. They basically intend to seek the true blessings of Divine through their most prized possession in the form of a beautifully adorned hair tattooed camel. Likewise, Ibn-Rushd (1126–1198), a prominent Muslim Philosopher popular as Averroes similar to Zuccari considered human senses may result in an erroneous creativity of humans. He quoted:

> Art is, in that sense, more limited than nature, given that art generates, within the quantities of colors that exist in the internal logos, only what the external logos is capable of producing. Meanwhile, nature produces all that there exists in the immaterial internal logos and that is why nature is nobler than art, and the nobility of the artist will depend on the degree of excellence with which he imitates nature, and this within the boundaries of the possible.[79]

It provides clear evidence that Ibn-Rushd considered the imitation of nature the only standard to judge a piece of art because of the reason that the act of God, that

---

[78]. Ibid., 6.

[79]. Valerie Gonzalez, *Beauty and Islam: Aesthetics in Islamic Art and Architecture* (London: I.B. Tauris Publishers, 2001), 18.

is nature, is free from anomalies while humans have limited sensibilities and skills to depict anything away from its mere representation. Similarly, the camel hair tattoo artist also thrives for depicting nature around him and puts no conscious effort to create anything inaccurate based from his own imagination without any link with the nature. He has firm belief that only God has the true intellect and spirit to show perfection manifested in His beautiful world of nature.

The art of camel hair tattoo not only deals with theosophy but the essence of spirituality has been significantly present in the symbolic compositions. The artist experiences while practicing, observing and even patronizing the hair tattoo art, the sense of spiritual ecstasy symbolized in the geometry of camel tattoo symbols. Similar intentions of old Muslim artists have been discussed in the *History of Muslim Philosophy* by M.M. Sharif (1893 -1 965) under the chapter "Painting" that,

> Islam came with a message that there is only one God, that He alone is worthy of worship, and that the forces of nature can be subjugated and bent to serve man's will and desire. It was necessary for Islam at that stage to subordinate the aesthetic to the moral, and the beautiful to the good. It was therefore, a historical necessity which led early Muslim to prohibit the art which fostered representations of god, goddesses, and natural heroes as objects of worship.[80]

Following the same moral objectives the camel hair tattoo artist employs geometrical and organic symbols to demonstrate his unique art and mystical affiliations. His main concern lies not just in beautification of his artistry but morality serves the supreme purpose behind the complex symbols of hair tattoos. In all honesty, the masters do not primarily produce intricately hair tattooed camels to raise finances for their modest life rather organize their cultural camel riding, racing or dancing activities without any cash rewards. The winners often get only a piece of white cotton cloth tied onto the neck of the victorious camels by the organizers as a symbol of pure celestial blessings and deep ancestral longings. The display of talents and bravery all serve the purpose of inner happiness of the Ruhilas with simple heartedness and openness. That has been the main reason thousands of Ruhilas visit the Sufi shrines every year along with their entire families including females and children in such tough weather conditions to show their intense devotion. The Ruhilas anxiously arrive on camels,

---

[80]. M.M. Sharif, *History of Muslim Philosophy* (Karachi: Royal Book Company, 2010), 1111-2.

bull carts, busses and motorcycles etc. and even bare foot on the burning and thorny sands of the desert to pay homage to their beloved Sufi saints singing holy songs and raising slogans in fervor of the respected Sufi.

These folks have been living in the desert for the past many centuries where they have been provided very little facilities. Truthfully, they still live in the ancient world that is deprived of all basic amenities but they live an astonishingly contented and satisfied life. They have no desire to shift to the city areas and even at times feel themselves more blessed than the people living in the developed cities. They claim to believe that in the urban areas people die early due to impure food and artificial medicinal products while they rely on having pure milk and butter provided by their beloved camels. Also, they believe themselves to be blessed with a peaceful life in the desert free of worries of the extraordinary living expenses that urban class has to incur. They prefer a simple domestic life for themselves and their children and learn the art of camel hair tattoo with a missionary zeal.

Similarly, the hair tattoo artist Gul Muhammad claimed that he is a disciple of Hazrat Pir Inayat Shah Bukhari and another saint who belongs to his neighboring areas of Chak 83 near Moj Garh Fort. He disclosed that the Sufis named Wallu Shah, Nawaz Shah and Tairak Shah came to meet him and gave him a *taweez* for his health and also prayed for his long life. He argued that he has been advised by his Sufi who lives in Mukdi near Channan Pir to offer prayers five times a day. He also send his boys to pay homage to the Sufi Channan Pir every year on the 7th Thursday of the Channan Pir festival. His sons also being camel hair tattoo artists start hair cutting of their camels on the first of lunar month in March every year to celebrate the arrival of the spiritual festivals. He believes that camel hair tattooing is a mystic practice that not all can achieve. Only those who have real dedication and commitment can learn to explore and master this art. In a question about the mortality of life Gul Muhammad argued that he strongly believes in life after death and no one has the power to run from facing death. He continued that the Creator on the Day of Judgement will gather us all and we will be answerable for our deeds.[81] He seemed quite satisfied in his straw house and was peacefully lying down on the *charpai* (a local bed) with a white shawl on him.

---

[81]. Gul Muhammad (camel hair tattoo artist) in discussion with the author, November 2013.

CHAPTER 5

The Symbols and Motifs of Camel Hair Tattoo Art

To focus the symbols of hair tattoo art we will begin with the Theory of Symbols proposed by Susanne Langer (1895—1985), an American philosopher who argued: "Symbol is an instrument of thought... A symbol or set of symbols works by communicating a *concept*, a general idea, pattern, or form." According to Langer, the concept is a meaning shared among communicators. The shared, agreed-upon meaning is the denotative meaning, and the personal image or meaning is the connotative meaning. Langer goes for the significance of *meaning* which relates symbol with its object and the person including both denotation (shared meaning) and connotation (the personal meaning).[82]

In the light of Langer's Theory of Symbols, the most important thing in the creation of symbols can be considered the thought process of the creative mind. The creative intellect is not only personally understood but also mutually understood by the whole community. Similarly, the artists of camel hair tattoo have commonly agreed upon using the Sun and the Moon symbols on the top of the camel humps to follow the setting of the universal order.

The humans are the only blessed creatures who have been awarded the power of intellect to understand the whole system of the universe. Karl Jaspers interpreted that "whole of the natural world is an encoded system of symbols to be deciphered by man."[83] Likewise, the camel artists have been struggling to interpret the symbols of heavenly bodies on their camels as the mystical devices to connect them with the celestial world of heavens. Furthermore, in the writings of German philosopher Immanuel Kant, *Critique of Judgment,* he defined symbols as "an indirect representations of the concept through the medium of analogy."[84] Therefore, symbols can be declared indirect depictions on the basis of the similarity they possess with the nature.

Symbols have been used by the humans since times immemorial. Laird Scranton (b. 1953) in his book *The Cosmological Origins of Myth and Symbols from the Dogon and Ancient Egypt to India, Tibet and China* wrote:

---

[82]. Stephen W. Littlejohn and Karen A. Foss, *Theories of Human Communication,* (Belmont: Thomson Wadsworth, 2008), 106.
[83]. Noth, *Handbook of Semiotics* (Bloomington: Indiana University Press, 1995), 116.
[84]. Ibid.,117.

> The very latest scientific work on the structure and genesis of matter, quantum theory and both string theory and torsion theory was known in very ancient times. However, it was and in some cases still is expressed in myth and symbol rather than in mathematical formulas.[85]

The study of the symbols used in ancient times reveals that the people had remarkable knowledge of science and religion. The ancient man was blessed with the scientific knowledge of cosmic structures and nature around him. We find that in the camel hair tattoo art the geometrical lines and shapes resemble the pre-historic caves paintings discovered in India. Also, the use of reddish color tone of henna dye look amazingly similar to the red-orange lines of the animals painted in the rock art (figure 35). The lines painted by the rock artists show division of lines following the body structure of the animal significantly along the shoulder blade. The similar division of lines can be observed from the shoulder blades of the tattooed camels found in Cholistan (figure 36). Interestingly, the tattooed camels found in Marut area of interior Cholistan desert exhibit horizontal, vertical and diagonal line patterns without the use of floral and vegetal motifs. It indicates that the desert artists of camel hair tattooing in interior Cholistan residing near the Pakistan- Indian border are still following their prehistoric ancestral links. The engraved parallel and vertical lines in the pre-historic caves of Khoupum District Tamenglong, Manipur, India also show great similarity with the lines of camel hair tattooing observed in the Marut (figure 37 & 38).

---

[85]. Laird Scranton, *The Cosmological Origins of Myth and Symbols From The Dogon and Ancient Egypt To India, Tibet and China*. (Vermont: Library of Congress Cataloging in Publication Data, 2010).

Figure 35. Deer in Red Ochre Colored Lines

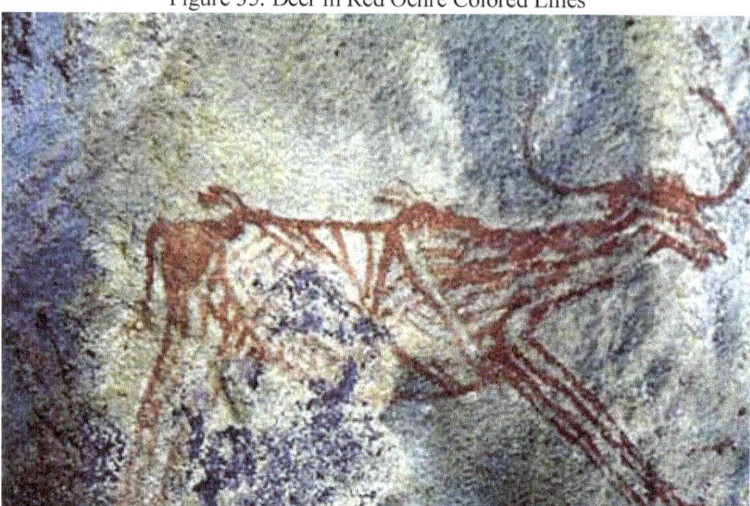

Source: Bhimbetka, Distrit Raisen Madhya Pradesh, India.
From Mesolithic Period resembling the lines and patterns of camel hair tattoo.
http://ignca.nic.in/asp/showbig.asp?projid=rock (accessed February 28, 2014)

Figure 36. Tattooed Lines resembling Painted Lines of the Rock Art

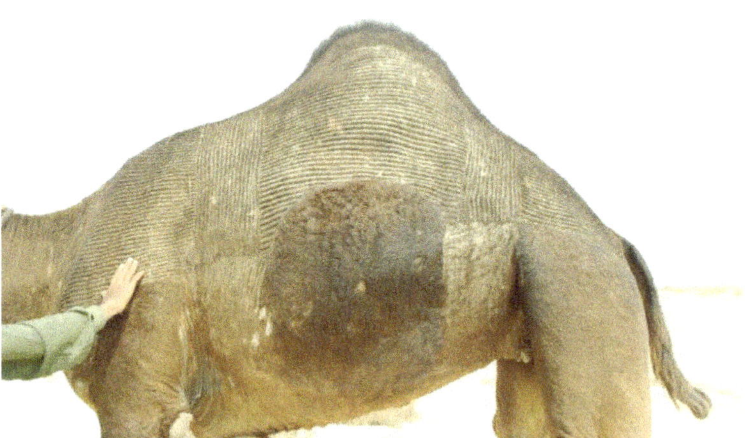

Source: Photograph by Muhammad Shafeeq, Marut, Cholistan 2014.

Figure 37. Engraved Parallel Lines of Rock Art

Source: Khoupum, District Tamenglong, Manipur, India. http://ignca.nic.in/asp/showbig.asp?projid=rock (accessed February 28, 2014).

Figure 38. Tattooed Lines resembling the Engraved Lines of the Rock Art

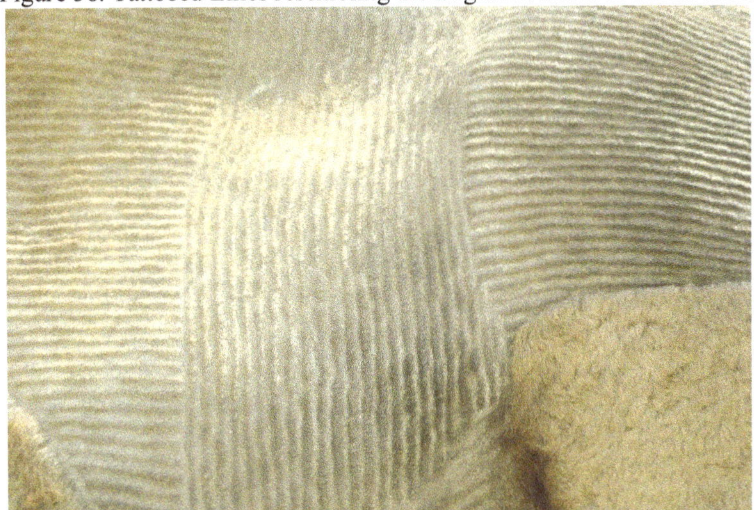

Source: Photograph by Muhammad Shafeeq, Marut, Cholistan 2014.

The ancient man pierced the skin all over the body and later the deep cut skin was filled with grinded pigments of various colors to enhance the effect of the tattooed designs. The geometric and floral lines and shapes followed the muscular body to beautify the curves and planes of the ancient man. Remarkably, similar notions of ancient man's tattoo designs can be observed in the deep hair cut lineation and formation of camel hair tattoo art. Later, with the development of religious sensibilities, an interesting metamorphosis developed from simple geometrical designs to the consecrated symbols which one can observe in the art of camel hair tattooing.

The humans living in the ancient civilizations of Egypt, Mesopotamia and the Indus Valley had acquired unique skills of architectural building, pottery making and astronomical calculations that all used geometrical figures. When millennia ago, Hakra River was flowing through the plains of Cholistan, it was an important part of the ancient Indus Valley civilization. The geometrical lines, shapes and forms used in the present day arts and crafts of Cholistan still carry the legacy of their ancestors.

The Greek mathematician Euclid around 300 B.C. gathered the knowledge of geometry and wrote extensively about it in the mathematical school at Alexandria. The treatise became available to the Arabs in the late eighth century to build for themselves the foundations of geometry in the Muslim art and architecture. The Muslim architecture included rhythmic figures and geometrical constructions perpetuated with symbolic, cosmological and philosophical findings. The geometrical designs played the most significant role in the development of the mystical dimensions in the building constructions and painted murals of the Muslim architecture. The Muslim artisan used the methods to construct designs which were not based on simple grids but had origin in the identical units repeated in the form of regular patterns. To create the basic divisions of the units, squares or hexagons were used with detailed patterns within them. The inner details helped to achieve proportional harmony with the other consecutive patterns progressing in various directions.[86] Therefore, the Muslim designs employed a sophisticated and mysterious symbolic language which was blended with the concept of a unified nature.

To uncover some mystical aspects of Muslim Art, we find that M.M. Sharif in his book on Muslim Philosophy has disagreed to call Muslim art as "erratic" and claimed that:

> For a Muslim, time and eternity are only two facets of the same reality; he does not have to create a dichotomy between time and eternity; he does not have to make time illusory in order to satisfy his longing for eternity. A Muslim is expected to try constantly to create eternity out of

[86]. Eva Wilson, *Islamic Designs* (London: British Museum Press, 2003), 15.

> time. No wonder then that Muslim painting tried to combine all dimensions in a single unity and all the phases of time in one whole.[87]

It shows that the Muslim artist intentionally does not rely on human perceptions rather strives for another world of mystic dimensions. Also, he ignores the third dimension, perspective and darkness of shadows in miniature paintings because he creates a world of his own which has little to do with the limited human perceptions and deals with the unlimited and eternal spiritual experiences. The geometry depicts the continuously changing elements of time to create one whole eternal world of a spiritual paradise.

Valerie Gonzalez in her book, *Beauty and Islam: Aesthetics in Islamic Art and Architecture* focused the significance of geometry. In the book, Ibn Haytham (965- 1040) popular as Al Hazen in the West, a prominent Muslim scientist was mentioned who contributed to the theory of optics which influenced European Christians in the Medieval and post Medieval Ages. The positivist thinker Robert Grosseteste (1175 -1253), quoted Ibn Haytham's teachings as:

> It is impossible to know nature without geometry: its principles are present in absolute within the whole universe and every part of it; it is through its lines, angles and figures that we have to represent all the causes of natural phenomena; without these means, it is impossible to reach the 'proper quid' in nature.[88]

In addition, Valerie Gonzalez in the book chapter "Abstraction, Kinetics and Metaphor: the 'Geometries' of the Alhambra" has discussed in detail the categories of Muslim geometry, its mathematical and conceptual aspects. She has discussed the numerous geometrical designs of the marvelous Alhambra which is a conjunction of complex Islamic geometrical variations. She quoted from the book *Rasail Ikhwan al-Safa* (Epistles of the Brethren of Sincerity):

> Geometry occurs in all the arts (sanai); every craftsman (sani), if he carries out measures in his art prior to proceeding to practice (amal), it concerns a type of theoretical geometry (aqliyya), namely the knowledge of dimensions and their content... Applied geometry consists of the

---

[87]. M.M. Sharif, *History of Muslim Philosophy,* (Karachi: Royal Book Company, 2010), 1113.

[88]. Valerie Gonzalez, *Beauty and Islam: Aesthetics in Islamic Art and Architecture* (London: I.B. Tauris Publishers, 2001), 23.

> knowledge of measures and its sense, and binding them to each other, being comprehended by sight (basar) and perceived (yudrak) by touch.[89]

Here, the geometry employed in art has been divided into two main categories, namely theoretical and applied. The theoretical one has been rooted in the cognitive sensibility while the applied one deals with practicality in terms of measurements and forms. Both the geometries vary on the basis of physical and non-physical qualities like the theoretical geometry covers the facts and digits of geometry on the basis of intellect while the applied one has a three dimensional quality to evoke the feeling of touch. Likewise, during the process of hair tattooing, the artist uses his sight to visually measure the motifs and symbols and their placement, and his sense of touch using his hands and fingers to create the intricacies in geometrical motifs. In particular, when he cuts with scissors in his dominant hand, he uses the index finger of the other hand to press the coarse hair to ensure even cutting.

To further study the geometry in Muslim Art we find that in the book, *Islam and Art* the author Lois Lamya Al-Faruqi in the chapter titled "Categories of Decorative Motifs" has divided the motifs of Muslim art into different categories. She discusses:

> One of these (decorative motifs) comprises the various types of abstract figures; the second includes all those motifs that can be classified as shapes from nature. Included among the abstract figures are three sub-categories: calligraphy, geometric figures, and non-geometric abstract shapes. The shapes from nature comprise three main subdivisions: vegetal motifs, animal and human motifs, and lifeless objects from nature. The last of these three is subdivided into motifs which repeat the stylized shapes of familiar objects and those resembling architectural components.[90]

Historically, the Muslim artists have a leaning towards calligraphy and, the use of geometrical and organic motifs in art and architecture. They had to adopt this expression of art because Islam forbids the depictions of animated imageries. Also, the camel hair tattoo artists too do not intend to use living imagery to remain within the boundaries of Islamic canons. If they ever have to depict some

---

[89]. Ibid., 75.

[90]. Dr. Lois Lamya Al Faruqi, *Islam and Art* (National Hijra Council, Islamabad: 1985), 121.

human portraits or animal figures they purposely stylize it to avoid any infringement of the Islamic injunctions.

Rightfully, M.M. Sharif portrays the feelings of the Muslim artist using circular forms as symbols. He goes:

> Muslim painting, consciously and unconsciously, employed symbols which represent mystical states. Sometimes endless curves with no beginning or end stand for the state for bewilderment in which nothing outside seems to gratify spiritual longings. At times mandala forms are used to indicate the state of spiritual wholeness which mystics desire to achieve. Western critics do not see these motifs in Muslim Art and like to dismiss it as merely decorative and ornamental.[91]

The investigation of symbolic and mystical art produced by the Muslims over the past centuries was never an easy task. One of the strongest reason is that the spiritual aspects of Islam are depicted in the form of geometrical symbols not in any recognized form of depicting living imagery. It is because of the fact that the central belief in Islam is in one God, the Powerful and the Absolute, who is invisible and is without any specific form. Whereas, the Western mind deals with its specified evaluations and verifications which often do not have any bearing for the spiritual belief on One unseen God of the Muslims.

In Islam, the prime belief in one God was depicted by Hallaj as three concentric circles of a *taweez*. The first concerned with God's external actions, the second their marks and third its consequences related to the creations. The central point is the *taweez* itself, knowledge at the foundation which is the knowledge of non-knowledge.[92] Similarly, the use of circle on square like the dome on a cubical structure is very common to Muslim architecture. It expressed the relationship of Heaven and Earth also perfection and imperfection. The complex forms cause a fresh change and a new movement and balance to allow the victorious hero or saint to pass through the classical triumphal arch. On spiritual level it depicts the saint who has achieved his spiritual goals and has shared closeness with God in honor of his holiness.[93]

The concept of Allah, the only One and Absolute led the absence of animated beings in the mosques of Muslims throughout the history. Very few instances of

---

[91]. M.M. Sharif, *History of Muslim Philosophy* (Karachi: Royal Book Company, 2010), 1114.

[92]. Jean Chevalier and Alain Gheerbrant, *The Penguin Dictionary of Symbols* (London: Penguin Books, 1996), 200.

[93]. Ibid., 197.

figurative mosaics and paintings are found at the palaces of Umayyads including Qaysar Amra and Khirbat al-Mafjar. But from the twelfth century, Muslims got involved in the use of figurative motifs in different artistic media. They images included the rich iconography of court life, images of musicians, drinkers, acrobats, hunting wrestling and bathing etc. having some Hellenistic influences. The style of depicting animated beings under the Seljuqs rulers was decorative but the realistic style was developed in Mesopotamia and Syria around thirteenth and fourteenth centuries.[94] Significantly, the exclusive vases contained the motifs of animals having geometrical designs within their bodies. The similar geometrical lineation can be observed in hair tattoo art. Therefore, the hair art of Cholistan can stand as a true bearer of truth that symbolizes the centuries old Muslim legacy without any shock of interference.

The camel hair tattooing artist translates his inner feelings in variously conceived and created ideograms. These creative forms include floral motifs, occasionally stylized animals and birds, and in rare cases abstract human portraits. The artistic treatment of these idioms is not of physical nature but of a paradisal nature which does not depict this earthly world but the beautiful world of paradise. This unique style acts as a gateway to the higher world by the virtue of its mysterious beauty. In the same vein, the hair tattoo artist attempts to exhibit the desert's paradigm of an ideal camel clothed in an incalculable phases of time and space.

Circle and Square

The form of a circle appears simple but has diverse qualities. It deals with the origin of life of both physical and spiritual worlds. The circle may depict an inner or outer entity on individual and collective levels. It mystically stand for infinity in its outer continuation of line without having any prominent end point. Its confinement is the beauty of a circle which encompasses the whole spatial format of the universe.

Proclus (410–485), a Greek Neo-Platonist, described circle as the symbol of Heavens and unity of the primordial elements. He mentioned that circle originated and returned to its center point from all its points on the circumference. Plotinus believed that the center of the circle was its origin. While the German Catholic priest and physician Angelus Silesius (1624–1677), who was famous for his mysticism and religious poetry, thought that circle was contained within its

[94]. *The Cambridge Illustrated History of the Islamic World* ed. by Francis Robinson, (Cambridge: Cambridge University Press, 1996), 258 & 272.

center. Also, the German Dominican mystic named Henry Suso (1300–1366) thought it depicted the relationship of God with creation. The circular movements of planets and representations in the Zodiac signs all showed expansion and harmony. That is the reason that many of the architectural forms are based on circle and its divisions. Plotinus asked himself about the circular movements of Heaven and replied himself that they all imitate the Intelligence. Furthermore, the primordial shape of circle was the projection of the sphere of World Egg. It represented the Earthly paradise in circle much is often depicted in mandalas. The drawn passage from circle to square in mandalas can be termed as a way from Earth to Heaven by the Chinese and further confirmed by Christians. In Hindu architecture, the transformations are from circle to square and from square to circle. The symbol of circle can stand for terrestrial mutability while the square expresses celestial immutability. Furthermore, the temples of the nomadic people were mostly built in circles which showed changing status while the settled societies construct square shrines.[95]

The circle also is the symbol of time in the form of a moving wheel. It expressed fullness and perfection in the ancient times of Babylonians who divided and subdivided the circle. The Christians symbolized the circle as eternity and the three overlapping circles were the Holy Trinity of Father, Son and the Holy Spirit.[96]

In Muslim traditions circle is the symbol of absolute perfection having no beginning or end. The Holy Kaaba is a black cube and pilgrims move around it in circular processions without any break in continuous movements. The ancient custom of circumambulation around the Sufi graves and places of sacrifice is largely practiced by the Muslims. In Persian literature the dome and wheel of heavens were commonly explored. The search of God was symbolized by the Sun and the circular movements of the planets around it. The great Sufi poet Jalal-al-Din Muhammad Rumi (1207–1273) wrote in the Mathnavi that he moved around with nine planets in every Heaven. The Persian Sufi poet Shaikh Mahmud Shabistari (1288–1340) in his Gulshan-i-Raz (The Secret Rose Garden) compared God with the form of a circle. Rumi differentiated the circumference of the physical world with the Circle of the Absolute Being. He also claimed that even the Sun and the planets circling around it can be found in a grain of sand when dissected.[97]

---

[95]. Jean Chevalier and Alain Gheerbrant, *The Penguin Dictionary of Symbols* (London: Penguin Books, 1996), 196.

[96]. Ibid., 197.

[97]. Ibid., 199.

Later, Carl Gustav Jung (1875-1961) an eminent Swiss psychiatrist who founded the analytical psychology described circle as an archetypal form of the whole psyche and of ego while the square depicts body and reality. He emphasized the vital role of abstract symbols like mandala (the Sanskrit word for circle) as an image of psychological divinity.[98] The symbols in expressing spirituality opened many doors for religious practices. The basic structure of a mandala is a circle that encloses a sacred space. It starts to become complicated when a quadrated form is placed in it. This sacred circle is found everywhere, in the Sun, the Moon, a flower, a face and an eye with a cross shape in it. The combination of squares and circles establish a relationship of opposites. The four directions of the cross fix the endless movement of the circle, which has no beginning or end. It is a symbol for the eternal whole, which transcends time and space. Also, it has been used as a meditative device for the past centuries.

Nearly all traditional designs of Cholistan carry circles in different ways proving circle as the fundamental element of the traditional patterns there. The circle also stands as a spiritual device and can be often seen tattooed on the hump of the camel. The color of henna is applied keeping in mind the basic structure of a circle, the mandala (figure 39). Yet the artist seems to understand it with reference to the shapes and patterns his ancestral masters have been observing for the past centuries. Interestingly, in Cholistan we come across many circular constructions of the houses using mud, bricks, straws and tree branches. The reason might be the same that circle represents the quickening power and changing status of the nomads. The camel hair tattoo artists also depicted circle on the top part of the shoulder blade to perhaps depict cosmic energy (figure 40). Also, there are engraved flowers from the rock art produced in Khoupum, District Tamenglong, Manipur, India (figure 41). The tattooed camel in the desert with symbols of circles on the body may symbolize to him a celestial being on the Earth.

---

[98]. Jean Chevalier and Alain Gheerbrant, *The Penguin Dictionary of Symbols* (London: Penguin Books, 1996), 197.

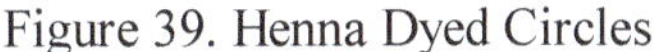

Figure 39. Henna Dyed Circles

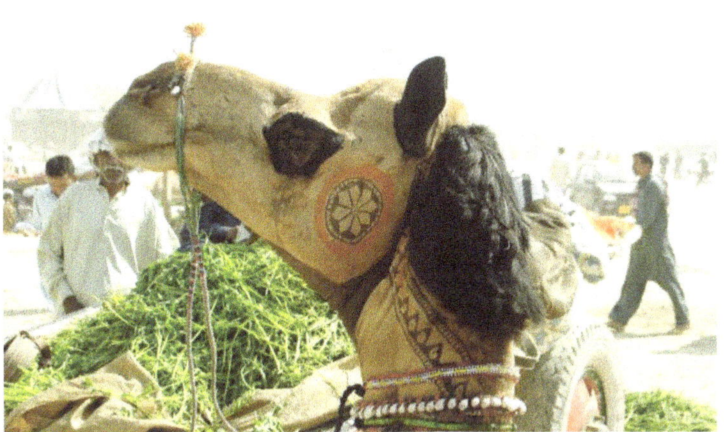

Source: Photograph by Muhammad Shafeeq, Channan Pir, Cholistan 2014.

Figure 40. A Circle formed by Camel Hair Tattooing

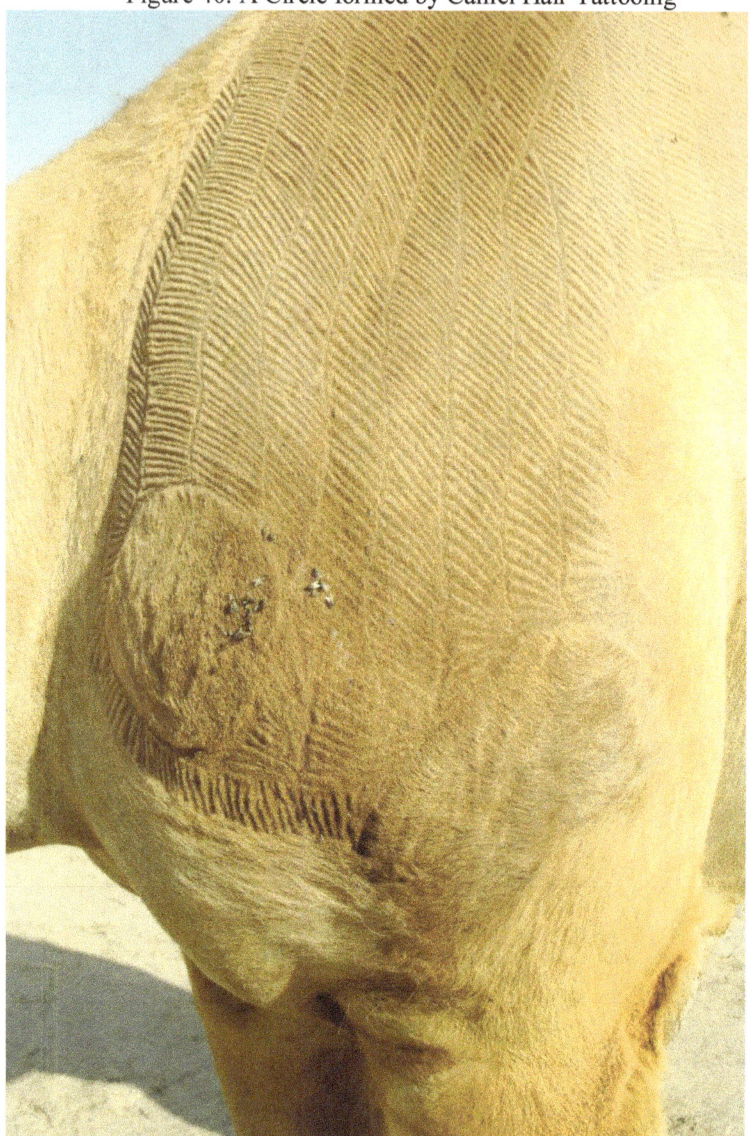

Source: Photograph by Muhammad Shafeeq, Channan Pir, Cholistan 2014.

Figure 41. Engraved Flower having a Circle

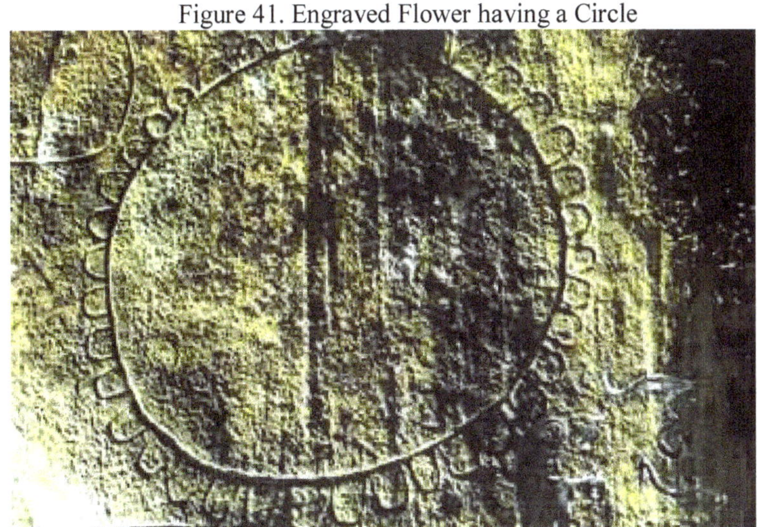

Source: Khoupum, District Tamenglong, Manipur

Engraved flower with a large circle in the center resembles camel hair tattooed circle. http://ignca.nic.in/asp/showbig.asp?projid=rock (accessed February 28, 2014)

TRIANGLE AND STAR

The German born American Gestalt psychologist Rudolf Arnheim (1904–2007) argued beautifully in his book, *Visual Thinking* about the visual data and the memory of a person to facilitate the understanding of symbols. He claims that the "visual knowledge and correct expectation will facilitate perception whereas inappropriate visual concepts will delay or impede it." A Japanese reads without difficulty ideographs as compare to the Westerner as he holds the characters in his visual storage. Similarly, "every break of the visual continuity between percept and memory norm also interrupts the dynamics connecting between the two. A bent figure attracts more of its characteristic expression through its visible pull towards and away from the norm of which it is perceived to be a deviation."[99]

Similarly, in the case of camel hair tattooing the variation of the bend and twist in the hair cut lines and forms manifest a distinct matrix. The visual data stored in the memory of the camel hair tattoo artist facilitates him to smoothly perform the task of cutting complex motifs and symbols of camel hair tattoo art. Just as a Japanese feels no problem in understanding the complex ideographs of their language as compare to a Westerner due to their visually stored knowledge. The hair artist uses the triangle shape more as compare to other geometrical

---

[99] Rudolf Arnheim, *Visual Thinking* (London: University of California Press, 1986), 95-96.

shapes to capture the attention of viewer. It may depict some influences of ritualistic and votive purposes favored by the Hindus worshippers in the ancient times.

A significant scholar of India, S.C. Saran in his article, “Teracotta Art Model of a Double-Edged-Axe Served as Votive Object from Maner (Bihar)” has investigated the ancient terra-cotta objects which belonged to at least 7th century B.C. They were rather used as toys and jewelry or may be for religious purposes. The author quoted that V.S. Agrawala has undoubtedly described Indian Art as the true reflection of Indian religion, thoughts, philosophy and culture. He explored the double-edged-axe from Maner, a small village on the west of Patna belonging to the Chalcolithic period. The nearby place from Maner has also showed traces of Neolithic era. Similar to the double-edged-axe different axes, swords, ornaments like bangles and rings with different anthropomorphic figures are also found in various areas including Balochistan, Pakistan. While in India, the discoveries were gathered from Haryana, Rajasthan and parts of Madhya Pradesh.

The double-edge terra cotta art model of Maner has five punctured triangular designs on one side and six on the other. The small sizes of the patterns suggested that they had not been used as weapons rather served votive, ceremonial and magical purposes. The same engraved triangles had been found repeatedly on the terra cotta seal of Antichak in which four triangles represented the tantric yantra. Also, the yantra comprised six triangles seen on the right side of the terra cotta art model of Maner. The basic shapes of triangles on these discoveries showed three worlds of neutral, negative and positive. The triangles pointing downwards represented the Yoni or female energy, the donor of nature and the triangles pointing upwards symbolized male principle. The two triangles with one another forming five pointed star had significant role depicting five elements of Earth, water, energy, air and Space.[100]

The god named Asura in Indian mythology is believed to have command on medicine and astrology. The investigation by the eminent Indian scholars, Ajit Mokerjee and Madhu Khanna mentioned in the book, *Recent Researches in Indian Art and Iconography* revealed that the two intersecting triangles in the form of a hexagon depicted kinetic energy regarding origin of life. The two interconnected triangles symbolized the Siva and Sakti the reason to the creation of whole universe. When these two triangles touch each other from apex points they manifest dissolution to cease the functioning of time and space. Similarly,

---

100. Dr. Bhagwant Sahai, ed. *Recent Researches in Indian Art and Iconography* (Kaveri Books New Delhi: 2008), 45.

Krishna Kumar explored the religious importance of five proto-historic painted patterns from Balochistan, Pakistan. He claimed that the triangle symbolized 'pudenda' the genital organ commonly of a female in painting from Mehi (Balochistan). In the region of both Pakistan and India it is significantly used as the symbol of fertility for worshipping since ancient times to date. The similar pair of triangles facing each other from apex had also been found on the heads of humped bulls and cows. It depicted the association of the male and female fertility bonding popular in the ancient world. Another yantra named Sri of modern Tantrika-worship is rooted in the pre-historic cult which employed the use of six triangles arranged within a circle.[101] Similar to the case of camel hair tattoo art, the zigzag lines facing each other in camel hair tattooing may stand as symbol of male and female union influenced by the ancient Hindu traditions. Although these lines do not resemble the real image of male and female figures. Likewise, Goodman has clarified that a symbol of an object has no limitation of resemblance with the object rather an unlimited set of symbols can be achieved depending on the thought process behind them. All symbols do not denote anything similar to the piece of abstract art. Still, abstract art has been considered a piece of art. Therefore, the piece of art does not necessarily represent anything existing in nature rather the thought process behind carries more weight.

An unlimited number of symbols are used in various cultures. These symbols discover the philosophical aspects of art to uncover the physical and the metaphysical vicissitudes. According to an eminent American art critic and philosopher, Arthur Danto (1924-2013), "It is our culture that interprets seen objects and thus adds meaning and significance to these perceived objects, telling us what these objects are to be seen as, but the objects seen are the same whatever interpretations we place on them.[102] Similarly, the art of camel hair tattooing can also be recognized with reference to its own cultural codes and the meanings it collectively generate.

The American author Clifford Geertz (1926–2006), the most significant anthropologist of his era, explored various dimensions of culture in his book *The Interpretation of Cultures*. In his book he discusses the views of the German sociologist Max Weber (1864–1920) as follows:

> The concept of culture I espouse, and whose utility the essays attempt to demonstrate, is essentially a semiotic one. Believing with Max Weber,

---

[101]. Ibid., 46.

[102]. Betty Conrad Adam, *The Re-emergence of Metaphysical Aesthetics: PhD Dissertation* (Houstan, Rice University: 1983), 70.

> that man is an animal suspended in webs of significance he himself has spun, I take culture to be those webs, and the analysis of it to be therefore not an experimental science in search of law but an interpretive one in search of meaning.[103]

Clifford Geertz also described in detail the significance of culture for the development of mankind. Clifford argued:

> Culture works as an interworked systems of construable signs (what, ignoring provincial usages, I would call symbols), culture is not a power, something to which social events, behaviors, institutions, or processes can be casually attributed; it is a context, something within which they can be intelligibly—that is thickly—described.[104]

It clearly meant that all cultures vary from one another and the standard of one cannot be applied on the other. The study of anthropology has facilitated to explore the meanings of interchangeable symbol systems rooted in their own particular cultures. Thus, the hair tattoo art on different camels seem to be closely interlinked with each other to form the unified symbols and motifs of cultural integration.

Interestingly, Marshall Segall and his associates analyzed that the people in backward rural areas can sense curved and slanted lines more accurately than the people who live in urban areas. This demonstrated that the rural and urban groups sense the nature differently as a result of their diverse cultural learnings.[105] Similarly, the art of camel hair tattoo observed in the interior desert of Cholistan areas display great mastery in using multiple quality lines following the body curves of the camel without any flora and fauna motifs.

The Ruhilas seem to be obsessed by the humble and gentle character of the desert ship having belief in his high level of understanding and intelligence. It might not have been easy to find any other place in the world except the desert of the subcontinent where the camels have been trained in such a vast range of activities including racing, riding, dancing, fighting, adventuring and displaying tricks. It clearly indicated that people from different cultures have different vocabulary of words and sounds. They have habits within their own cultural

---

[103]. Clifford Geertz, *The Interpretation of Cultures: Selected Essays* (New York: Basic Groups, 1973), 5.

[104]. Ibid., 14.

[105]. "Culture's Influence on Perception," 61, http://www.sagepub.com/upm-data/45975_Chapter_3.pdf (accessed November 22, 2014).

boundaries without any compulsion of following the footsteps of any other community. The variations between the habits and its understandings all urge us to recognize the indigenous arts in their own mystical, cultural and referential codes. Similarly, all the cultures comprise their specific standards and choices originating from their own actions and gestures. Fred E. Jandt in his book, *An Introductiion to Intercultural Communication: Identities in a Global Community* quoted under the headings, "The Greeks Had Aristotle and the Chinese Had Confucious" that:

> Nisbett (2003) and others contend that Eastern and Western cultures literally perceive different worlds. Modern Eastern cultures are inclined to see a world of substances—continuous masses of matter. Modern Westerners see a world of objects—discrete and unconnected things. There is substantial evidence that Easterners have a holistic view, focusing on continuities in substances and relationships in the environment, while Westerners have an analytic view, focusing on objects and their attributes.[106]

In addition, Rabindranath Tagore (1861–1941), the Indian artist, poet and philosopher, argued in his essay "What is Art" that a non-artist who if asked to draw some object will just follow the outline and copy the real thing but an artist over looks all details and gets into the essential portrayal. When he looks at the tree, he observes the real personality of it not just its representation. The Indian mind always believed that everything has a soul which the artist explores in his own inner self. He describes:

> The greatness and beauty of Oriental art, especially in Japan and China, consists in this, that there the artists have seen this soul of things and they believe in it. The West may believe in the soul of Man, but she does not really believe that the universe has a soul. Yet this is the belief of the East, and the whole mental contribution of the East to mankind is filled with this idea. So, we, in the East, need not go into details and emphasize them; for the most important thing is this universal soul, for which the Eastern sages have sat in meditation, and Eastern artists have joined them in artistic realization... [107] We have often heard the Indian

---

[106] Fred E. Jandt, *An Introductiion to Intercultural Communication: Identities in a Global Community* (California: Sage Publications, 2012), 59.

[107] G. N. Devy, ed., Indian Literary Criticism: Theory and Interpretation (New Delhi: Orient Blackswan, 2002), 146.

> mind described by the Western critics as metaphysical, because it is ready to soar in the infinite... Therefore it has come out so profusely in her symbolism of worship, in her literature. [108]

The similar intention of the universal soul of the East has been reflected in the symbolism of camel hair tattooing. That involves no artificial or materialistic approach but rather an observation in the purest form. The artist undergoes a pure spiritual experience much like a sage without the aid of the conventional materials. The simplicity of the tender motifs of camel tattoo art depicts the realization of The Truth, The Divine and The Creator.

The artist Jam Abdul Wahid, who is well-known for showing performances of his dancing camels, was interviewed at the traditional camel riding competition of Latan Har Shinghar. He referred to some native terminology commonly used by the camel hair tattoo artists of Cholistan which includes *gudra* and *kingra* meaning zigzag and curved lines respectively (figure 42). Also, *katta* refer to the triangle and *tukri* is diamond-cut shape (figure 43). They shapes are much liked by the camel hair tattoo artists with the motifs of leaves and branches called *bail* for further beautifications (figure 44).[109] The triangles and curved lines of camel hair tattoos show great similarity with the rock paintings of Madhya Pradesh (figure 45). Also, the children of Cholistan play named *gharwa* in which they jump on one leg on the different geometrical shapes drawn on the ground (figure 46). These games have ancient tradition depicted in the various prehistoric rock art sites including the Shibee River Valley which is a newly discovered rock art site in the neighboring Rajasthan, India (figure 47). Interestingly, the mark making of this game is similar to the ancient prehistoric and Chalcolithic rock art in Samadha Hill, India (figure 48).

---

[108]. Ibid., 147.

[109]. Jam Wahid (camel hair tattoo artist) in discussion with the author, November 2013.

Figure 42. G*udra* Zig-Zag and K*ingra* Curved Lines

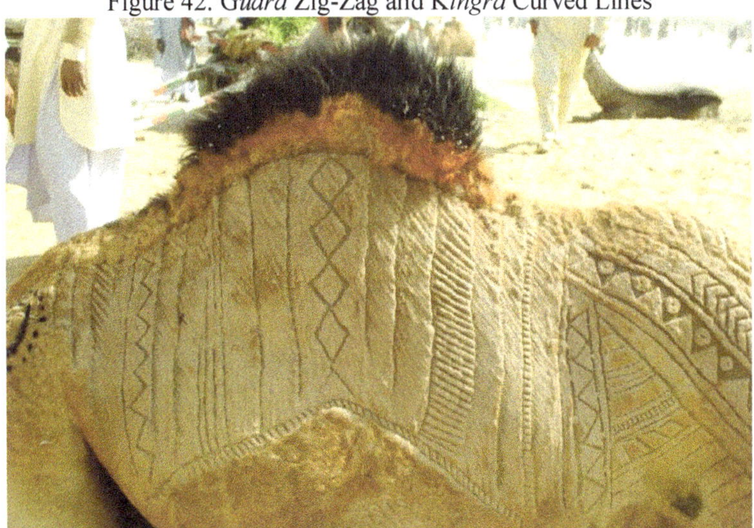

Source: Photograph by Muhammad Shafeeq, Channan Pir 2014.

Figure 43. Heer cutting *Katta Triangles* and *Tukri* Diamond Shapes

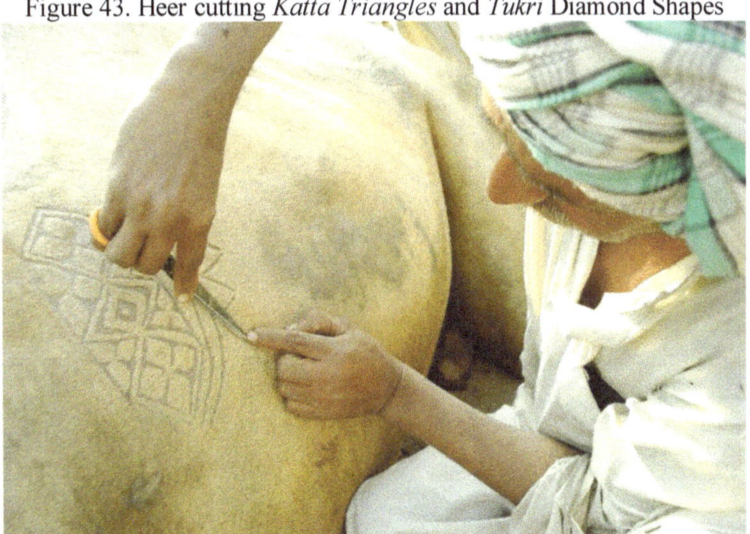

Source: Photograph by Muhammad Shafeeq, Ahmad Pur 2014.

Figure 44. *Bail* Motifs

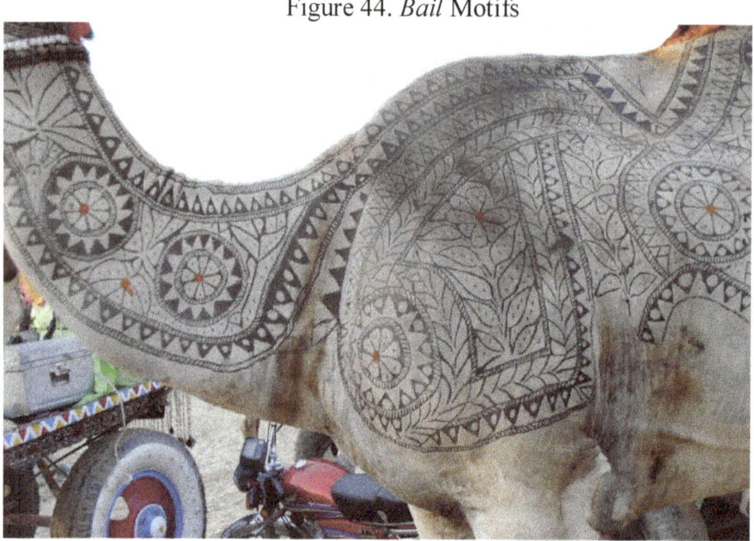

Source: Photograph by Muhammad Shafeeq, Ahmad Pur 2014.

Figure 45. Triangular and Curved Bands

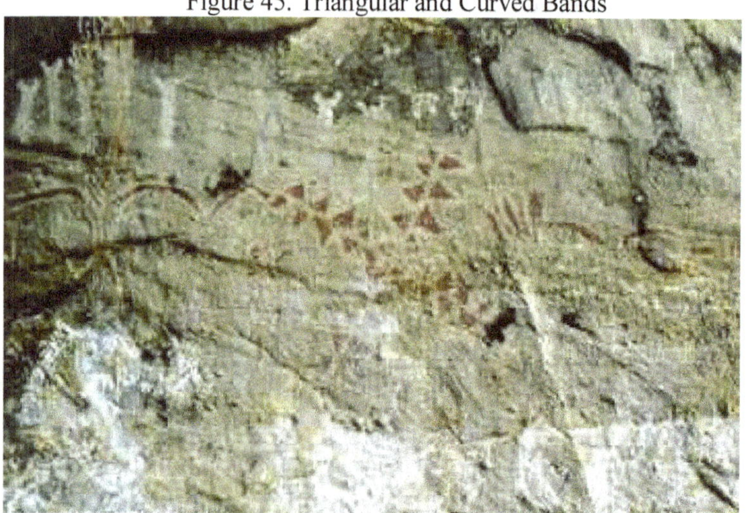

Source: Madadev, District Pachmarhi, Madhya Pradesh.

Triangles in red and white colors with curved lines resemble Katta and Gudra patterns. http://ignca.nic.in/asp/showbig.asp?projid=rock (accessed February 28, 2014).

Figure 46. Cholistani Children Playing *Gharwa*

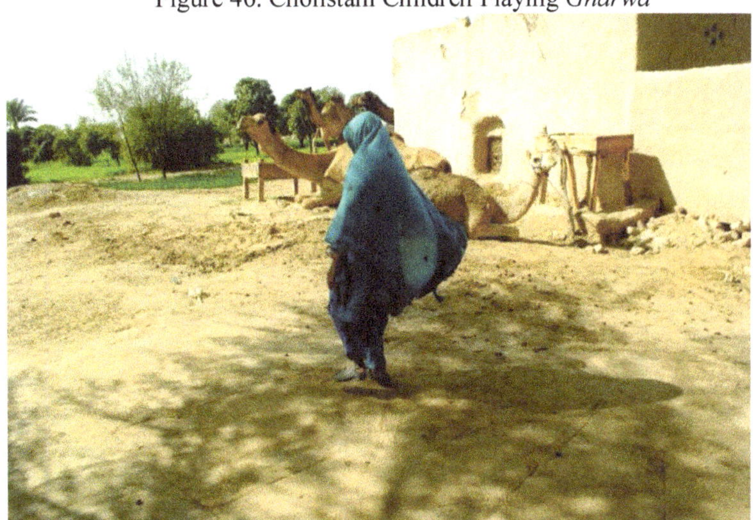

Source: Photograph by Muhammad Shafeeq, Miranian 2014.

Figure 47. Engraved Game Board

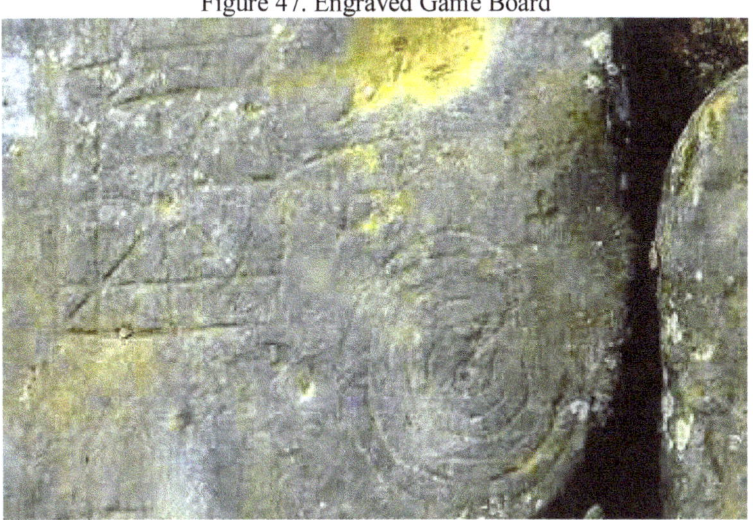

Source: Khoupum, District Tamenglong, Manipur.
The game board show similar divisions of the playing activity of Cholistan.
http://ignca.nic.in/asp/showbig.asp?projid=rock (accessed February 28, 2014)

Figure 48. *Gharwa* Playing Activity depicted in Rock Art

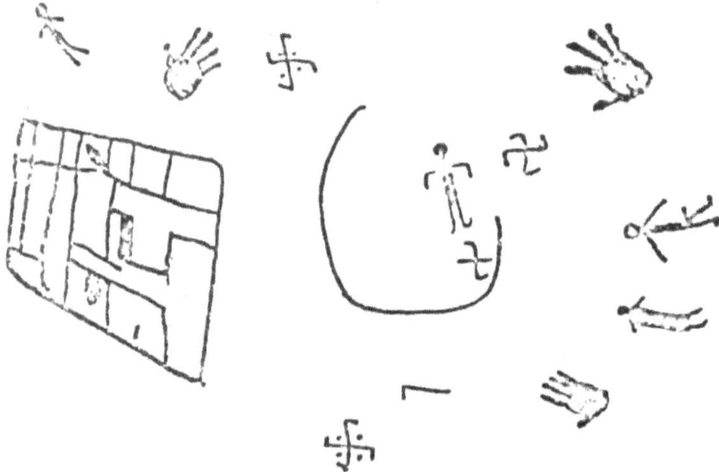

Source: Samadha Hill: Chalcolithic (2m x 2cm).
Photograph taken from the book, Recent Perspectives on Prehistoric Art in India, page 158.
The mark making shows resemblance with the mark making of the game named gharwa played in Cholistan.

The most prominent shape in the art of camel hair tattoo is that of a star (figure 49). It is vividly used by the hair tattoo artists due to its significant role in the life of Cholistani people. Since it had been difficult to travel in the hot desert during the day time, these folks used to travel on camels at night and found the right direction and distance to their destinations with the help of some stars. They had a profound interest in astrology, and they observed the stars very carefully to calculate the best time for marriages. They used the positions of the planets and the stars to predict the fate and good omen. This esoteric knowledge is still surviving among these Ruhilas.

The oldest surviving artist of camel hair tattoo art near the Moj Garh Fort, Gul Muhammad who was discussed earlier in the chapter, "The Distinct Artists of Camel Hair Tattoo Art" disclosed interesting facts about his ancestors who used to document dates on dried out leaves by counting the number of sun rises, moon appearances at night and observing the star constellation movements. He claimed that they could accurately guess the time of night by observing the constellation of the seven stars. He further added that the stars served as a navigational guide to the people of Cholistan particularly the prominent *Dubai* (sic.) star that shines in the direction of north.[110] Clearly, the constellation of seven stars that Gul Muhammad alluded to was the Great Bear and the *Dubai* star could only be the North Star. The word *Dubai* is corruption of *Dub-e-Akbar* which is the Arabic term for the Great Bear. In English it is also called Dubhe.

Figure 49. Cosmic Symbols depicted on the Hump

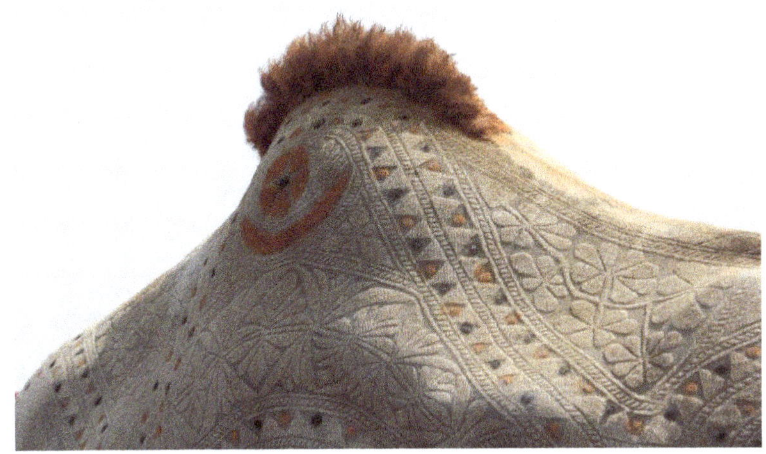

Source: Photograph by Muhammad Shafeeq, Channan Pir 2013.
Five Pointed Star with the Sun and a Crescent

Following the traditions, the astronomical symbols including the Sun, the Moon, and the stars depict the metaphysical order of the universe for the camel hair tattoo artist. The social, religious and artistic aspects were all amalgamated in the rhythmic patterns of these universal bodies. Gul Muhammad revealed that he often liked to depict the star shape with variables of 4, 5 and at times 7 points on the hump of the camel. He himself also likes to compose it with the crescent shaped moon.[111]

The shape of star has been depicted with various other motifs and patterns in camel hair tattoo art. Most frequently it is depicted with the floral pattern placed within it (figure 50). The stars vary in sizes and numerals depending on the form of body it is placed on. The dominant parts of the camel including the humps and shoulder blades carry star marks. The whole body of the camel having star symbols and dots with red and black dyes may symbolize the days and nights

---

[110]. Gul Muhammad (camel hair tattoo artist) in discussion with the author, November 2013.

[111]. Gul Muhammad (camel hair tattoo artist) in discussion with the author, November 2013.

(figure 51). Generally, star is believed to be symbol of Divine blessings therefore, it is not tattooed on the lower parts of the camel. The reason is often discussed by the camel hair tattoo artists that star is a sacred symbol for them and should be tattooed on the higher parts of the camel showing the universal settings of these heavenly bodies.

Figure 50. Details

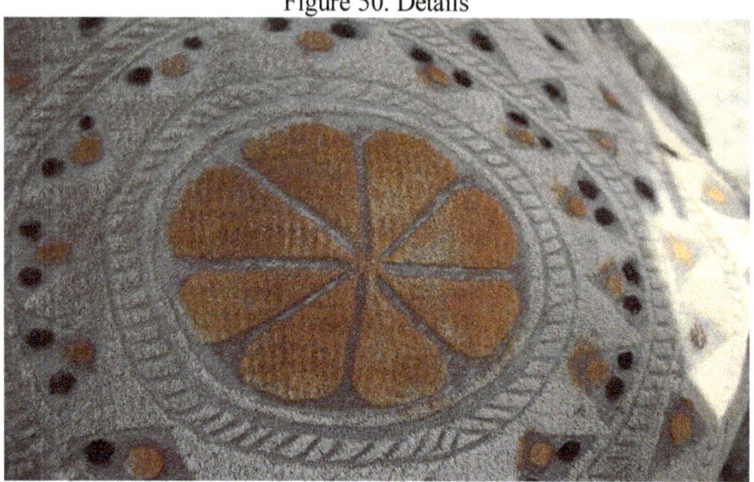

Source: Photograph by Muhammad Shafeeq, Channan Pir 2013.

Figure 51. Cosmic Symbols

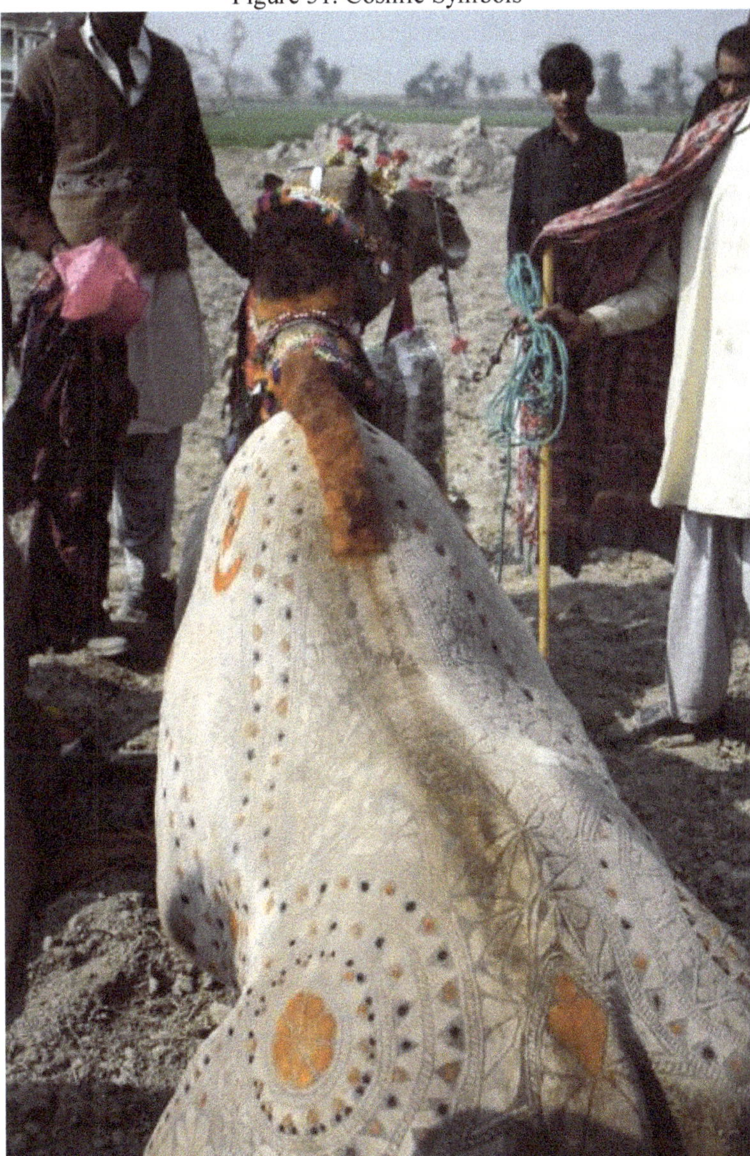

Source: Photograph by Muhammad Shafeeq, Channan Pir 2013.

One of the most liked and repeatedly used shape in camel hair tattooing is that of a floral motif. It is often used within the star symbols having different number of petals. The petals of the floral motif change according to the body forms and contours of the camel. The prominent body area of the camel is often highlighted with floral motifs of eight petals whereas the other areas show flora of six petals (figure 52). The flowers stand as a symbol of spring season for them which is warmly welcomed with traditional festivals of religious and secular nature in Cholistan. The petals of the floral motifs resemble the star motifs painted in the rock art of Chambal, Madhya Pradesh, India (figure 52) which located at about a distance of 1200 kilometers from Cholistan.

Figure 52. Floral Motif encircled with Fourteen Pointed Star

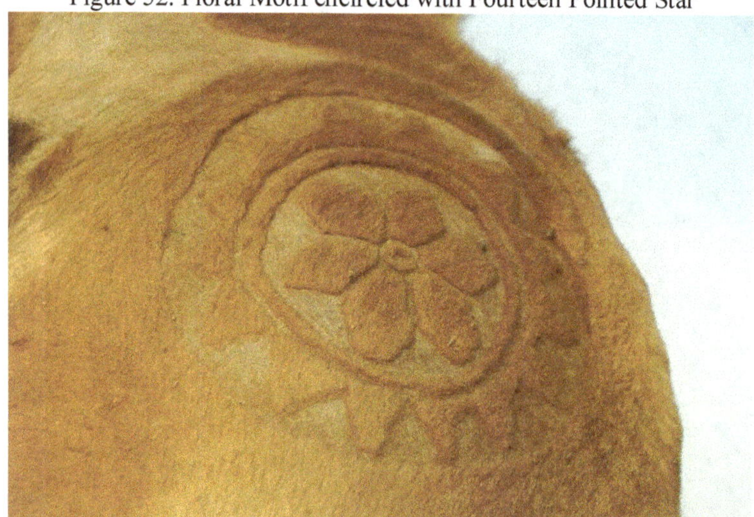

Source: Photograph by Muhammad Shafeeq, Latan Har Shinghar, Cholistan 2014.

Figure 53. Star Symbols in Rock Art

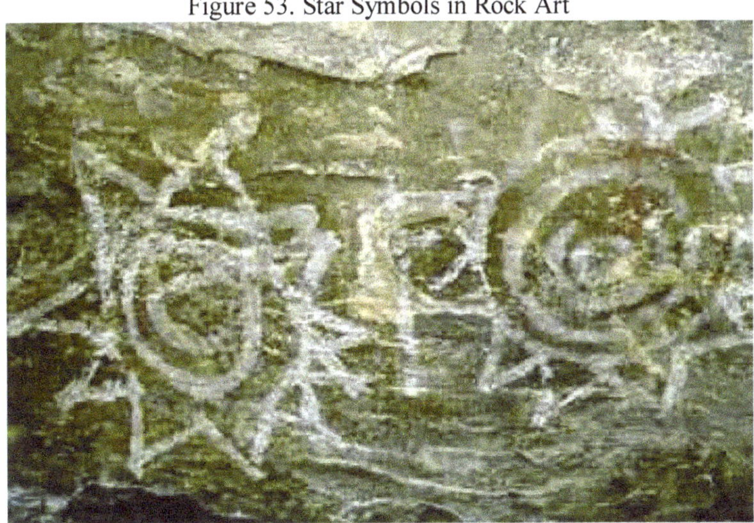

Source: Chambal, Madhya Pradesh.

Two Star Symbols are painted in white color similar to the floral tattoos. http://ignca.nic.in/asp/showbig.asp?projid=rock (accessed February 28, 2014).

In a paper by Mohammad Shafeeq Chaudhry, he mentioned some artistic inspirations of camel hair tattoo artists to depict the local vegetation namely butterfly weed, leafs of dish cloth gourd, garlic plant leaves and *korwal da pita* (a local name), a Cholistani herb of *kadu di wal* with rarely used motifs of abstract animals, birds, and human figures.[112]Also, Gul Muhammad, the tattooing artist of Moj Garh village informed about the leaves of betel, butterfly weeds and henna plant which he often likes to use in his hair tattoo art (figure 54).[113] Also the vegetal inspirations mentioned earlier by Iqbal Dhaya including sponge gourd (*tori*) motifs, date plant (*khajur*) motifs, betel leaf (*paan*) motifs, cypress (*saru*) motifs and calotropis (*aak*) motifs. Calotropis flower is five petalled and resembles five pointed star motifs etc. All are different inspirations of nature in Cholistan.[114]

---

[112]. Mohammad Shafeeq Chaudhry, "The Art of Camel Hair tattoo in Cholistan, Punjab, Pakistan." International Journal of Scientific and Research Publications, Volume 4, Issue 9, September 2014, http://www.ijsrp.org/research-journal-0914.php (accessed February 26, 2014).

[113]. Gul Muḥammad (camel hair tattoo artist) in discussion with the author, November 2013.

[114]. Iqbal Dhaya (camel hair tattoo artist) in discussion with the author, November 2013.

Figure 54. A Heart Shaped Motif

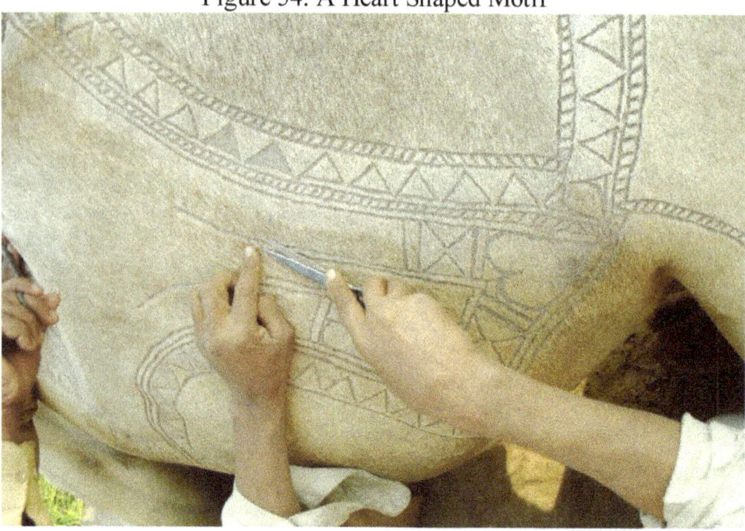

Source: Photograph by Muhammad Shafeeq, Ahmad Pur, Cholistan 2014.

Similarly, Khawaja Ghulam Farid also mentioned some of the beautiful vegetation of Cholistan translated in English as:

You are my beauty and my fate, fortune, fame.
You are my looking, enquiring, seeking
You are my understanding, my knowing
You are my henna, my collyrium,
My rouge, my tobacco, my betel-leaf![115]

The native Sufi of Cholistan seems greatly influenced by the desert beauty just like the other habitants of Rohi significantly the camel tattoo artists. Similar to the Ruhila artists of camel hair tattooing, Khawaja Farid used the elements of nature like the henna, betel-leaf and collyrium to create beautification and feminism in his poetry.

The artist of camel hair tattooing is using the above mentioned plants and leaves with additions of floral motifs (figure 55). He is deeply observing the geometrical forms of the leaves and composing them within the format of the camel's hairy body (figure 56). The artist feels no intention to depict the vegetal

---

[115]. "Sufi Poetry: *Meda Ishq Vi Toon/* Khawaja Ghulam Farid," https://Ṣūfipoetry.wordpress.com/2009/11/03/meda-ishq-vi-toon/ (accessed December 2014).

motifs realistically but wants to show his inner feelings and spiritual longings rooted in Islam. At times, the patrons of camel hair tattooing show desires for depicting stylized animal motifs. Following the wishes of the patron, the master of camel hair tattoo art swiftly draws the animal motif with ordinary stationary marker and later cuts it with great mastery (figure 57). The animal motif is cut in abstract manner to depict feelings and emotions of the people of Cholistan. The camel motifs show various camel activities including the aggressive camel fighting. The camels show orange and black color which may symbolize the good and evil forces (figure 58).

Figure 55. Betel Leaf Motifs

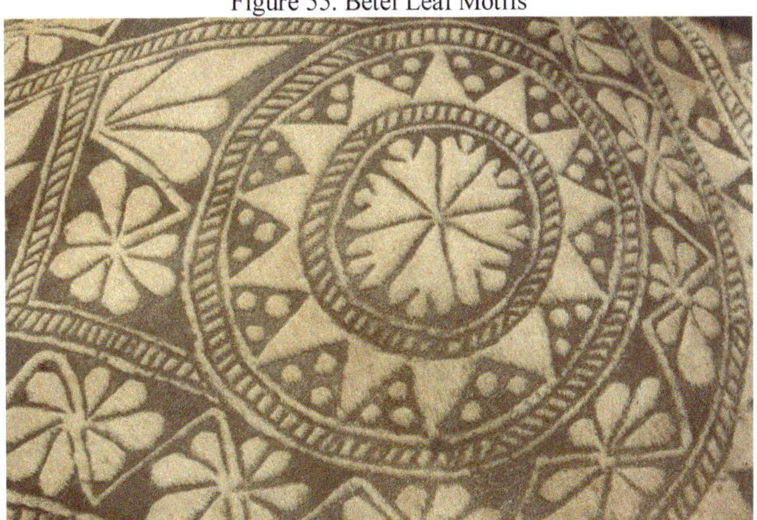

Source: Photograph by Muhammad Shafeeq, Ahmad Pur, Cholistan 2014.

Figure 56. Organic Symbols and Motifs

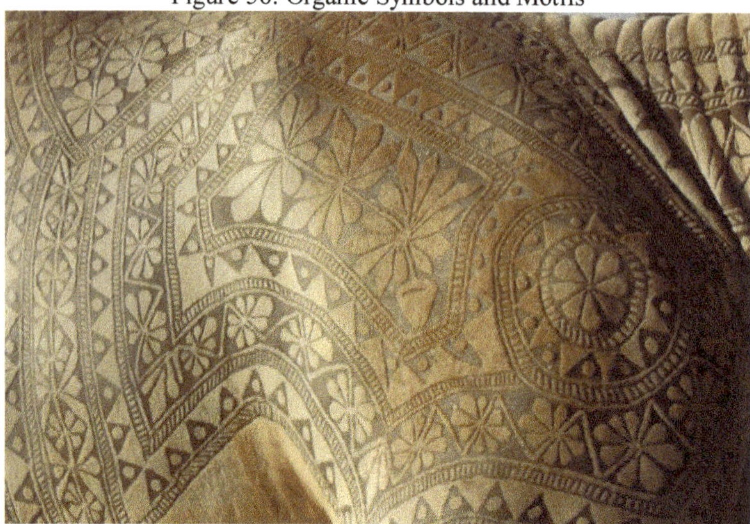

Source: Photograph by Muhammad Shafeeq, Ahmad Pur, Cholistan 2014.

Figure 57. Drawing of an Abstract Camel

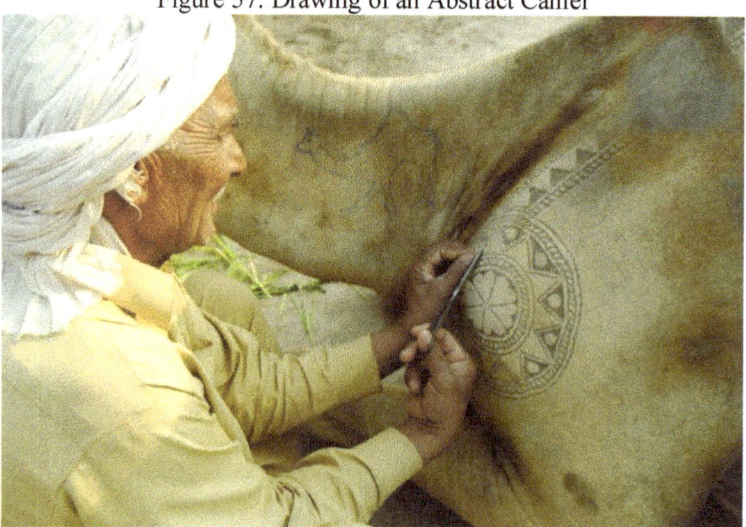

Source: Photograph by Muhammad Shafeeq, Ahmad Pur, Cholistan 2014

The preliminary drawing of a camel observed on the neck of camel

Figure 58. The Good and Evil Camel Fighting Motifs

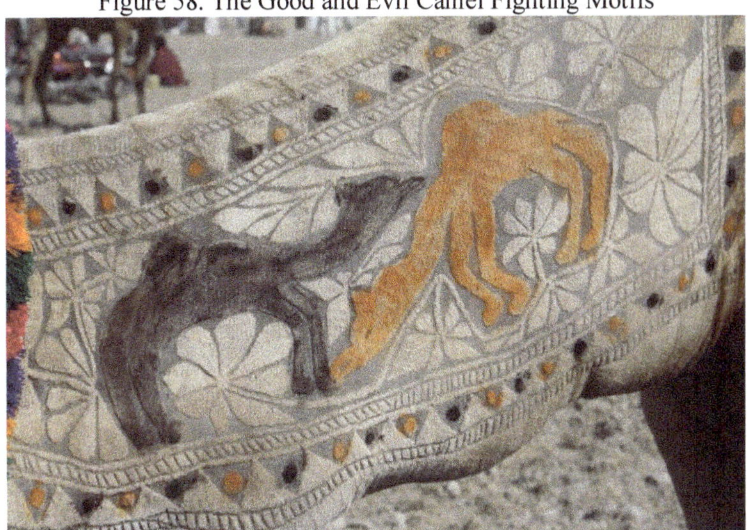

Source: Photograph by Muhammad Shafeeq, Ahmad Pur, Cholistan 2014

The similar range of motifs can be observed frequently in the numerous traditional arts and crafts of Cholistan like pottery and its painting, tie and dye, block printing, textile embroidery, patch work of *ralli* (bed sheets), *parandah* (head dress), *changair* (plate made from date-palm leaves), *khussah* (traditional leather shoes), and *huqqa* (hookah—the traditional smoking instrument) etc. These traditional objects carry various geometrical and floral motifs which are amazingly similar with each other. Undoubtedly, the artists and artisans of Cholistan have used diverse geometrical shapes in their traditional arts and crafts. The art of camel hair tattooing is an obvious blend of finely cut shapes which greatly resemble the traditional bed sheets (*ralli*) of patch work. These beautiful pieces of colorful cloth are used to cover the tattooed camels to accentuate their mystifying beauty (figure 59).

Figure 59. The *Ralli* Textiles

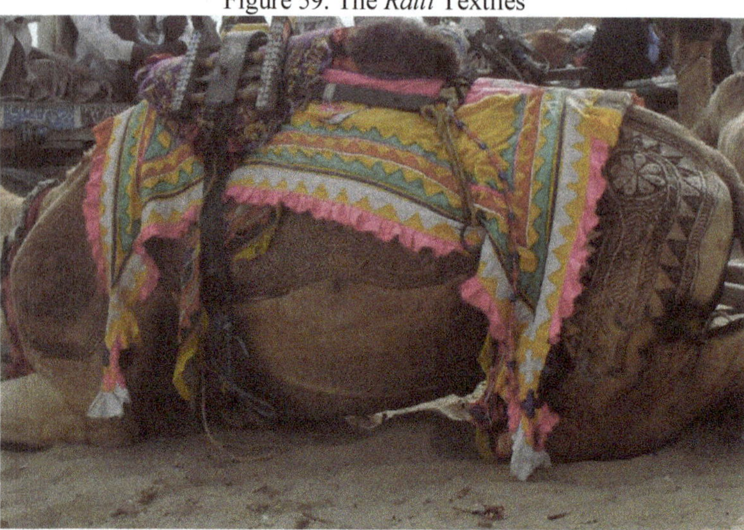

Source: Photograph by Muhammad Shafeeq, Channan Pir, Cholistan 2014.

The fascinating tattooed camel exhibits its beauty in the open environs of sandy dunes and ridges of Cholistan. In fact, the ordinary carts of camel and ox are also richly decorated with the traditional patterns comprising triangles, squares and circles. Even the hand fans also carry similar patterns of triangles on its fringes like that of the traditional plate (*changair*) made from date palm leaves (figure 59 & 60). Wherever one moves around in Cholistan, these triangles, circles and squares follow as a mystical longing morphed into the traditional display of artistry. The artist of camel hair tattoo art seems to be obsessed with these geometrical conventions and just cannot separate himself from them.

Figure 60. Traditional Hand Fan

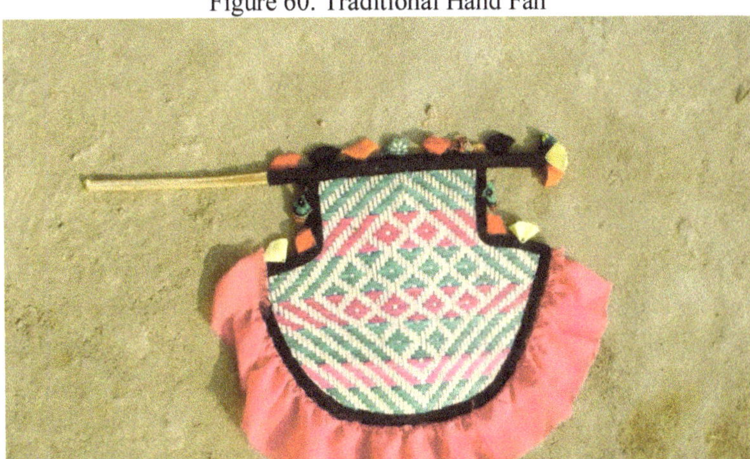

Source: Photograph by Muhammad Shafeeq, Ahmad Pur, Cholistan 2014.

Figure 61. Traditional Plate made from Date Palm Leaves

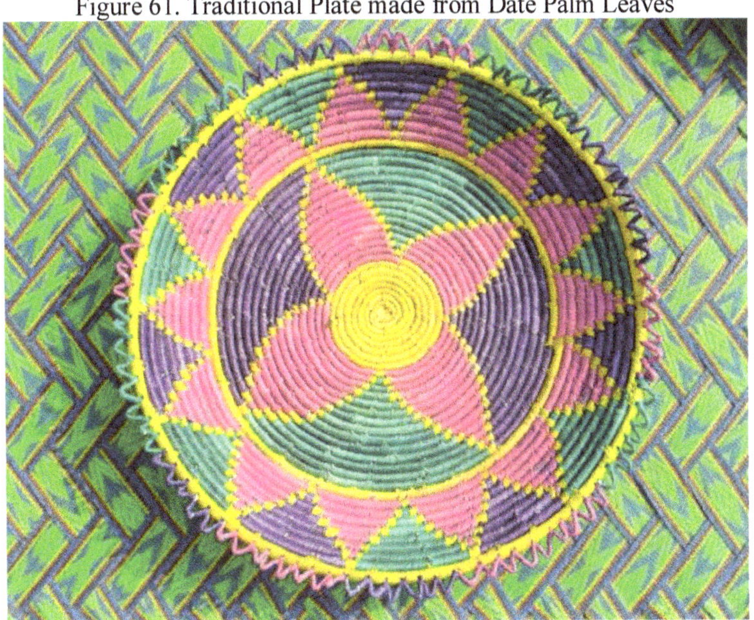

Source: Photograph by Muhammad Shafeeq, Ahmad Pur, Cholistan 2014

CHAPTER 6

Epilogue

The diverse meanings of symbols in the art of camel hair tattoo unveil an extra-ordinary artistic and philosophic mind of a true artist. The camel hair tattoo practice of Cholistan has deep and mystical roots in art, spirituality and religion. The camel hair tattoo symbols reveal Islamic mysticism, the characteristics of Muslim artistic legacy also some influences of ancient Hinduism. In addition, Muslim philosophy, the symbol theories, cultural and traditional leanings seem to be an unconscious derive of the camel hair tattoo artist. All these spiritual and philosophical findings verifies the reason to call it a unique art form of Cholistan, Pakistan.

In fact, the investigation itself was not an easy task as it deals with the subjects, styles and techniques of different artists of camel hair tattoo without any documented records. The reason may lie in the fact that the Ruhilas of Cholistan are mostly illiterate nomads and pastoralists and have little literary leanings and there has been no significant effort made by them or others to preserve their past or present in books. They seem to follow the oral traditions of their ancestors in learning the art of camel hair tattoo and have no intention of recording this beautiful art form. The supervision and guidance of the mystics and the saints of Cholistan have molded their personality without any intention to work for worldly fame. The Ruhilas of Cholistan, whose lives are marked with a lifelong struggle in the desert, have an innate ability to explore beauty and peace around themselves. This is what brings beauty and meaning to their lives and makes life easy and joyous. The diseases of the modern times like anxiety, depression and hypertension are non-existent there. They are the poorest of the poor but nevertheless, there has been no reported case of suicide which is an indication of fulfilment and contentment in their lives.

The best part of the year for the Ruhilas to relax and rejuvenate is the spring season when they enjoy the moderate weather after intense winters. This is the time for them to beautify their most beloved possession—the camel, which they do by cutting the hair of the camel in a unique way. They take care of their camels like their own off-springs and spend much of their savings on their adornment. The adorned camels then accompany them to the shrines of their Sufi saints to seek the spiritual enlightenment. Their art for them symbolizes their love and devotion to Allah to achieve spiritual ecstasy.

The cutting of the hair of a gigantic herbivore in the form of multiple geometric and organic nature carries significant meanings. When the hair tattoo artist is busy embellishing the camel with beautiful motifs, he is totally absorbed in his work, oblivious to the world around him, seeming as if to be in a trance. This requires the dedication of a true artist which meekly mortals with impoverished spirituality and shallow intellect cannot undertake. Everything transcends unto him in the form of various artistic and mystic symbols. On close observation, these magnificent constructions spreading all across the camel's body convey the intuitive messages of the traditional, cultural and religious norms, The camel hair tattoo artist seems to be deeply influenced by the artistic ancestry of the subcontinent.

Some of the geometric lines and symbols used in camel hair tattoo have been found much similar to the geometrical lines used in the pre-historic rock paintings in India. Significantly, the agricultural phases of the Indian cave man showed animal figures covered with the geometrical lineation is similar geometry of camel hair tattoo symbols. Also, the ancient Indus Valley pottery has vegetal and geometric patterns that resemble the floral and geometric symbols of camel hair tattoo art in Cholistan.

The desert of Cholistan was one of the earliest places in the subcontinent which were introduced to Islam. There are still some Hindu settlements in Cholistan but only the Muslims practice the art of camel hair tattoo. They are dedicated to their religious doctrine and they purposely keep themselves away from hair cutting or painting animated figures. Only a few instances show bird and animal motifs but they too are articulated in the form of abstraction.

Only a few decades ago, the camel hair tattoo artists were not in the habit of using artificial art materials. For example, when they needed a brush to apply the henna dye on the camel they chewed a side of thin and soft branches of the trees to prepare handmade brushes for the purpose. Similarly, the artificial black dye of Kala Kola was not much favorably used in those times. Lately, the modern brushes and hair dyes have been introduced to ease the complex process of hair cutting and painting.

The marks of henna on the camel's body look like the brush strokes of a painter. These marks express a sense of spiritual purity. The range of rhythmic hues of henna from yellow to almost black show the day and night, good and evil, body and spirit of the Ruhila which is on a constant search of the Truth. The Truth that is reflected in his every hue and cry of Cholistan.

The hair tattoo artist depends heavily on his personal drive and inner satisfaction. On close observation the individual style in every camel can be assessed with subtle variations of hair cutting and patterning. The symbols of five pointed star and the crescent as well as the presence of vegetal motifs and abstract birds and animals used in camel hair art all show the artist's intellectual, cultural and religious aptitude and commitment with the Islamic doctrine.

To analyze in depth the spiritual aspects of camel hair tattoo art, an attempt is made to search references of the camel in the sacred books of the Holy Quran, Vedas, and the ancient Manu Scriptures. The verses from the religious scriptures belonging to Aryans, and Hindus helped to conclude that the old inhabitants of the subcontinent knew about the camel. It has been mentioned as a symbol of power of the God in ancient Yajur Veda of the Aryans. The second mantra of Kuntap Sukt in the Atharvaveda also showed traces of camel but for the riding of a prophet. In the Holy Quran, the verses also highlight the she-camel as a sacred symbol of Divine mercy. On the contrary, the ancient Hindu scriptures of Manu-smriti (11:201) and Manu Samhita proves that the camel has been forbidden for the Hindu Brahmans which mark the most elite class of the Hindu Doctrine.

The camel being taken as a despicable animal the Hindu clergy and its absolute absence in any form of the ancient Hindu art and even the Buddhist art of the subcontinent confirm the probability that camel art of hair cutting might have been introduced or at least propagated by the Muslims.

The study of camel hair tattoo significantly revealed that the life of a Ruhila orbits around the most respected figure of his Sufi sage. He puts all his efforts to make him delighted and attentive for seeking the holy blessings. The preparation of his beloved and sacred possession in the form of an ostentatious camel reveals mystical phases of time. The centuries old lineage of not only artistic depictions but spiritual devotions of the Muslim artist is rejuvenated in the forms of allegorical geometry of camel hair tattoo art.

The philosophy in art has facilitated to call art as an accomplished process of self-exploration and in the last one hundred years or so has replaced its perspective of imitating beauty with an intellectual creativity. The artist's thought and style of self-expression has achieved prime importance leading to the multi-dimensional ways of experimentations. Interestingly, these stylistic expressions of not only creating images rather breaking down the images have won an equal appreciation. Furthermore, an abstract piece of art can be considered superior over realistic art depending on its level of allegorical creativity. This exploration helped in the development of symbols which directly influences the thought processes and intellect of men. The role of culture and tradition is very dominant in this regard and must be considered the standards of measuring art and intellect. Here, in this study significant arguments have been put forward which show ample proof of declaring the art of camel hair tattoo a true invoice of an artist and its hair tattooed camel a sculpted object.

An interesting observation has been made that as we move from the periphery of Cholistan to its interior we see both the motifs and the lifestyle of the people become simple showing a direct relationship with each other. This could perhaps be explained by the fact that the people living in the interior are less privileged, face more hardships, and are less exposed to the variety and glamour of modernity. This provides an interesting avenue for further research into this interesting aspect of the behavior of the Ruhilas towards art.

The hair cutting art involves high risk to the artist because of direct contact with the small hair particles spreading in the air. The health hazards, changing trends and high financial demands have discouraged the hair tattoo artist to teach the precious art to their loved ones and are now bound to send their young ones to school.

Like other aspects of our lives this exuberant art is also losing its purity of spiritualism, depth of intellect and lineage with the past. The art is expanding from the commercial point of view but is losing its purity and soul.

References

Adam, Betty Conrad. *The Re-emergence of Metaphysical Aesthetics: PhD Dissertation*. Houstan, Rice University: 1983.

"Animal Figure at Bhimbetka." India Netzone: Indian Monuments, Bhimbetka, Madhya Pradesh. http://www.indianetzone.com/10/bhimbetka.html (accessed February 28, 2014).

Arnheim, Rudolf. *Visual Thinking*. London: University of California Press, 1986.

Auj, Nurul Zaman Ahmad. *Harapan Heritage*. Multan: Caravan Book Centre, 1998.

Bigwood, J. M. *Ctesias' Indica and Photius.* http://www.electronicsandbooks.com/eab1/manual/Magazine/P/Phoenix%20CA/1989/Bigwood%20-%201989%20-20Ctesias'%20Indica%20and%20Photius.pdf (accessed March, 7, 2015).

Chaudhry, Muhammad Shafeeq. "The Art of Camel Carving in Cholistan, Punjab, Pakistan." International Journal of Scientific and Research Publications, no. 9 (September 2014). http://www.ijsrp.org/research-journal-0914.php (accessed October 25, 2014).

Chaudhry, Muhammad Shafiq and Umer Farooq, "Camel Rearing in Cholistan Desert of Pakistan," Pakistan Veterinary Journal, no. 29 (2009). http://pvj.com.pk/pdf-files/29_2/85-92.pdf (accessed August 20, 2014).

Chevalier, Jean and Alain Gheerbrant. *The Penguin Dictionary of Symbols.* London: Penguin Books, 1996.

Craven, Roy C. *Indian Art: A Concise History*. London: Thames and Hudson, 2001.

"Culture's Influence on Perception." http://www.sagepub.com/upm-data/45975_Chapter_3.pdf (accessed November 22, 2014).

Devy, G. N., ed. *Indian Literary Criticism: Theory and Interpretation.* New Delhi: Orient Blackswan, 2002.

Erdosy, George, ed. *The Indo-Aryans of Ancient South Asia: Language, Material Cultural and Ethnicity.* Berlin: Walter de Gruyter, 1995.

Fadiman, James and Robert Frager, ed. *Essential Sufism*. New Jersey: Castle Books, 1998.

Faruqi, Dr. Lois Lamya Al. *Islam and Art*. Islamabad: National Hijra Council, 1985.

Forbes, Robert Jacobus. *Studies in Ancient Technology*. Leiden: Library of Congress, 1965.

Gommans, Jos. *Mughal Warfare: Indian Frontiers and High Roads to Empire 1500–1700*. London: Routledge, 2002.

Gonzalez, Valerie. *Beauty and Islam: Aesthetics in Islamic Art and Architecture*. London: I.B. Tauris Publishers, 2001.

Goodman, Nelson. *Languages of Art: An Approach to a Theory of Symbols.* Indiana: Hackett Publishing, 1976.

Graham, Gordon. *Philosophy of the Arts.* New York: Gordon Graham, 1997.

Geertz, Clifford. *The Interpretation of Cultures.* New York: Basic Groups, 1973.

Hameedi, Mansoor, Muhammad Ashraf, Al-Quiany, Tahira Nawazi, Muhammad Sajid Aqeel Ahmad, Adnan Younis and Nargis Naz. Medicinal Flora of the Cholistan Desert no. 43 (December, 2011). http://www.pakbs.org/pjbot/PDFs/43 (SI)/07.pdf\ (accessed December 14, 2014).

Hendrix, John Shannon. "Humanism and Disegno: Neoplatonism at the Accademia di San Luca in Rome," School of Architecture, Art, and Historic Preservation Faculty Papers. no. 1 (2007). http://docs.rwu.edu/saahp_fp/1 (accessed October 8, 2014).

"India Netzone: Indian Monuments, Bhimbetka, Madhya Pradesh." http://www.indianetzone.com/10/bhimbetka.html (accessed February 28, 2014).

Khalid, Samia and Aftab Hussain Gilani, "Distinctive Cultural and Geographical Legacy of Bahawalpur," Pakistaniaat: A Journal of Pakistan Studies, no. 2, (2010), 13, http://pakistaniaat.org/index.php/pak/article/download/62/62 (accessed February 25, 2015).

Littlejohn, Stephen W., and Karen A. Foss. *Theories of Human Communication.* Belmont: Thomson Wadsworth, 2008.

Mughal, Muhammad Rafique. *Ancient Cholistan: Archaeology and Architecture.* Lahore: Ferozsons, 1997.

Noth, Winfried. *Handbook of Semiotics.* Bloomington: Indiana University Press, 1995.

"Prophetic Timeline: Life of Prophet Muhammad S.A.W.W." https://prophetictimeline.wordpress.com/2011/03/26/the-conquest-of-makkah-year-8ah/ (accessed November 13, 2014).

Rehman, Atta ur. Fawad Khan, Marcus Moench, Sharmeen Malik, Lea Sabbag & Karen Mac Clune. "Desk Study: Indus Floods Research," http://r4d.dfid.gov.uk/pdf/outputs/CRISSA/Indus_Floods_Research_Appendix_5.pdf (accessed May 12, 2013)

"River Saraswati or Saravati." http://manashsubhaditya.blogspot.com/2012_01_22_archive.html (accessed January 15, 2015).

Robinson, Francis. ed. *The Cambridge Illustrated History of the Islamic World.* Cambridge: Cambridge University Press, 1996.

Sahai, Dr. Bhagwant. Ed. *Recent Researches in Indian Art and Iconography*: New Delhi: Kaveri, 2008.

Scranton, Laird. *The Cosmological Origins of Myth and Symbols From The Dogon and Ancient Egypt To India, Tibet and China.* Vermont: Library of Congress Cataloguing in Publication Data, 2010.

Sharif, M.M. *History of Muslim Philosophy*. Karachi: Royal Book Company, 2010.

Sharma, R.K. and K.K. Tripathi, ed. *Recent Perspectives on Prehistoric art in India.* New Delhi: Aryan Books International, 1996.

Segall, Marshall H., Donald T. Campbell and Melville J. Herskovit, "The Influence of Culture on Visual perception," in Social Perception, ed. Hans Toch and Clay Smith. http://web.mit.edu/allanmc/www/socialperception14.pdf (accessed September 28, 2014).

Surah Al-A'rāf, Al-Quran, Verse 73. http://Qur'ānindex.net/kelime.php?id=7984 (accessed November 21, 2014).

Surah Hūd, Al-Quran, Verse 64. http://Qur'ānindex.net/kelime.php?id=7984 (accessed November 21, 2014).

Surah Al-Isrā, Al-Quran, Verse 59. Http://Qur'ān.Com/17/59 (accessed November 21, 2014).

"Sufi Poetry: "Meda Ishq Vi Toon, Khawaja Ghulam Farid." https://Sufipoetry.wordpress.com/2009/11/03/meda-ishq-vi-toon/ (accessed January 10, 2015).

Sunnan-i abi Dā'ūd: trans. Volume 42, Hadith 4784. http://sunnah.com/abudawud/43/30 (accessed November 12, 2014).

Swidler, Ann. "Culture in Action: Symbols and Strategies," American Sociological Review 51, no. 2 [Apr 1986].

http://www.jstor.org/stable/2095521 (accessed August 18, 2014).

Littlejohn, Stephen W. and Karen A. Foss. *Theories of Human Communication.* Belmont: Thomson Wadsworth, 2008.

"The Vedas: An English-only, Indexed Version of the 4 Veda Smahitas in One Document." https://zelalemkibret.files.wordpress.com/2012/03/the-4-vedas.pdf (accessed January 27, 2015).

Thompson, Wentworth, trans. *History of Animals* http://pinkmonkey.com/dl/library1/gp007.pdf (accessed July 18, 2014).

Unal, Ali. *The Prophet Promised.* New Jersey: Tughra Books, 2013.

Wilson, Eva. *Islamic Designs.* London: British Museum Press, 2003.

Wilson, Horace Hayman. *Notes on the Indica of Ctesias.* Collingwood: Collingwood printing, 1836.

INDEX

D

E

F

G

H

I

J

K

O

P

Q

R

S

T

U

V

W

Y

Z

www.ingramcontent.com/pod-product-compliance
Lightning Source LLC
LaVergne TN
LVHW020511100826
845148LV00003B/754
9781612298894